KT-451-627

William

Dressage Formula

Erik F. Herbermann

Dressage Formula

SECOND EDITION

Foreword to first edition by Egon von Neindorff

J. A. ALLEN
LONDON

First edition published 1980
Reprinted 1984
Reprinted 1986
Second edition, completely revised and re-set, published 1989
British Library Cataloguing in Publication Data
Herbermann, Erik F.
    Dressage formula. – 2nd ed.
    1. Livestock.: Horses. Riding. Dressage. Manuals
    I. Title
    798.2'3

ISBN 0–85131–486–4

Published in Great Britain by
J. A. Allen & Company Limited
1 Lower Grosvenor Place
London SW1W 0EL
Printed in Great Britain

Preface to the Second Edition

Since it first appeared, in 1980, *The Dressage Formula* has gone through several reprintings. The gratifying enthusiasm with which it has been received has prompted me to produce this second, fully revised and expanded edition. It represents an ever continuing search for finding better ways of imparting the heart of this fascinating subject to all those who love the horse.

This new book has been divided into two parts. Part I is based on the same concise format of the original edition. However, besides numerous additions, it contains a further detailed distillation of concepts down to their root elements in an attempt to achieve yet greater clarity. Part II consists of a number of essays that have been added to complement the terse skeletal structure of Part I. This layout has been used so that the reader can choose either to review specific points quickly or, when more time allows, can elect to browse through the longer chapters at leisure.

The detailed essays in Part II entail both technical and philosophical aspects of horsemanship: the meaning and use of the aids; the correlation between attitudes of the seat and position and their effects on the horse; and last, an essay on the nature of art.

Though many of the pictures from the first *Dressage Formula* still appear in this new volume, illustrations of the finest examples of correct work have now been included. These portray performances of some of the most highly respected horseman from the past.

With this book I wish to share those things which I have found to be of value, and hope that it will be of assistance to all dedicated scholars of the horse, not only in identifying and avoiding some of the common pitfalls which can plague every rider, but especially to help keep the valid ideals and standards of horsemanship alive in our times. Let's study the horse together.

ERIK F. HERBERMANN
Gambrills, Maryland, December 1987

Contents

Correct attitude and driving influence from the
seat.
Incorrect attitudes and driving influences of the
seat and position.
What is a weight aid?
Timing of the driving aid from the legs.
Important factors about activating the horse.
Indications of the horse's acceptance or rejection
of the aids.
Tuning the horse to aids from the seat and legs.
Quality of the rein contact.
Quality, quantity and intonation of the aids.
Sequence of changing position and aids when changing
the rein.
Essential points for correct bending.
REFLECTIONS

Principles of riding.
Six major guidelines for correct riding and training.
Fundamental aims in training the horse.
Framing the horse.
Framing function of the seat.
Criteria for the correct head position of the horse.
Completion of the circuit.
'On the aids' – versus – 'collection'.
What does 'on the aids' mean?
How is the horse put 'on the aids'?
Forward and down.
Equal loading of the horse's legs.
REFLECTIONS

Categories of exercises.
Practical use of exercises.
Elaboration on the loosening exercises.
Elaboration on the suppling exercises.

Purity of the gaits.
Incorrect work.
Signs of tensions or incorrect work.

Acknowledgements

I would like to thank my friends and instructors who over the years have contributed significantly to my education both as a person and as a horseman. I wish to include special recognition to those who have generously spent many hours of guidance, especially at the time when I could hardly have been considered anything other than a stumbling beginner. Often such individuals are overlooked because they happen not to be among the ranks of 'world-renowned masters'.

Those who have contributed most significantly are: Mrs. Patricia Salt, FBHS., who taught, with precision and correctness, that art of riding that she herself had learned at the Spanish Riding School, and from her studies with Richard L. Wätjen. Others who assisted during these early years were, Heidi Hannibal and Monty Smith. Further, it was through Dietrich von Hopffgarten that I was accepted as a working pupil at the Reitinstitut von Neindorff in Karlsruhe, West Germany. I was greatly influenced by Mr. von Hopffgarten's riding, which he demonstrated during several clinics which I attended, and am most grateful to him for his contribution of explicit examples of fine horsemanship which radiated such undeniable qualities of competence and truth.

I am particularly deeply indebted to Mr. Egon von Neindorff, from whom I have been able to glean the bulk of material upon which I have built my equestrian experiences. It has been a unique education to have worked under the guidance of this knowledgeable, artistic Master.

I wish to express my appreciation to Mr. John R. Pullen for going over the final drafts of this book, and offering his most helpful critique.

All photographs representing the author's work were taken by George A. Ross. The X-ray shots were made possible through the kind assistance of Mr. & Mrs. Kenneth Giles, and were taken by Janice Kneider, and Dr. N. Brown, Chief Radiologist.

The photograph of the ballerina, Galina Samsova, is reproduced by the kind permission of Anthony Crickmay, and is from his book *Dancers* published by William Collins.

The photographs of Richard L. Watjen and Öberbereiter Meixner are from Richard Watjen's book *Dressage Riding*, published by, and reproduced by permission of, J. A. Allen & Co.

Ludwig Koch's drawing is from his book *Die Reitkunst im Bilde*, Vienna, 1928.

Leonardo da Vinci's drawing, 'The Apostle Phillip', from the Royal Collection at Windsor Castle, has been reproduced through the gracious consent of Her Majesty Queen Elizabeth II. This sketch is from Leonardo's studies for his famous fresco 'The Last Supper', which is located in the refectory of the monastery of Santa Maria delle Grazie in Milan, Italy.

Finally, I wish to thank Mr. J. A. Allen, and the professionals of J. A. Allen & Co., Ltd., for the special care they have taken to produce this second edition of *Dressage Formula* so beautifully.

It is with deep regret that I add to these words of acknowledgement the names of two deceased friends whom I dearly loved, and regarded most highly both as human beings and as horsemen: Walter B. Thiessen, and Dan A. A'haroni.

Walter B. Thiessen, August 7, 1937–July 31, 1981. Walter was a soft-spoken unassuming person, and a gentleman in every way. He was a highly respected trainer in Cutting Horse circles throughout North America. He had a way with horses the like of which I have seldom seen since. His influence on me regarding the general handling of horses will always remain a vital part of my horsemanship.

Dan A. A'haroni, November 7, 1939–November 5, 1984. Dan was a highly intelligent, sensitive, and honest person, whose encouragement and constructive criticism were most helpful to me in producing the first edition of *The Dressage Formula*. It was through his assistance that the book was first published. As a horseman Dan was unwavering in his search for the classical ideals, and uncompromising in his attempts to put them into practice.

Vorwort *(foreword to the first edition)*

Herr Erik Herbermann hat in sein mehrjärigen Aufenthalten an meinem Karlsruher Institut nicht nur reiterliches Können gezeigt. In einer Zeit des schnellen Wechsels und ständiger 'Umwertung der Werte' bewies Herbermann Klarheit und ungenwönliches Einfülungsvermögen mit der Beständigkeit, die seine Arbeitsweise auszeichnet. Das kam der erfreulichen Fülle fachlicher Kenntniss und praktischer Erfahrun sehr zugute, die in seinem Buch niedergelegt sind.

Die anschauliche Art der Darstellung, erläutert mit vielen instruktiven Bildaufnahmen aus der Arbeit des Autors, spricht den Leser als Freund der gemeinsamen Sache ebenso an wie die Probleme der täglichen Praxis. Sorgsamer Aufbau der Ausbildung von Pferd und Reiter ist der Grundzug dieses Bekenntnisses zur reellen, dauerhaften und vielseitigen Basis reiterlicher Erfolge.

So wünsche ich diesem Buch weite Verbreitung bei allen, denen die Probleme der Reiterei unserer Zeit mit Ernst am Herzen Liegen.

EGON VON NEINDORFF

Foreword (translation)

During his many years' stay at my Riding Institution in Karlsruhe, Mr. Erik Herbermann has not only displayed equestrian ability. In an age of rapid changes and continual 'alteration of values', Herbermann demonstrated a clarity and unusual perception for constancy which distinguish his method of work. This has come to good stead in the gratifying abundance of professional knowledge and practical experience which have been laid down in his book.

The attractive mode of presentation, which is illustrated by many instructive photographs of the author's work, relates to the reader as a friend in both general matters as well as the problems of daily practice. Careful construction in the training of horse and rider is the characteristic of this Creed for a real, enduring and diverse basis of equestrian success.

Thus I wish this book a wide propagation to all those who seriously take to heart the problems of riding in our times.

EGON VON NEINDORFF

Preface to the First Edition

This book contains an organized documentation of ideals and standards of fundamental academic dressage riding. It is a summary of my findings, based on a meticulous and critical study of the long-established principles of horsemanship, which I have diligently attempted to apply in both training and teaching.

This work does not pretend to be a replacement for the excellent literature written by the Great Masters. The basic concept is by no means new. The reason for this book is primarily to be a concise theoretical support: as a preparation for instruction, or one's daily riding sessions, leaving these free to be fully utilized for their rightful purpose – the translation of theory into practice.

The emphasis of the text is singularly aimed at accuracy, brevity, clarity and objectivity. The headings of all sections are numbered for the purpose of cross-referencing, to avoid tedious repetition or redundancy.

THE DEFINITION OF DRESSAGE

Dressage is the methodical, gymnastic training of the horse. It is based upon the three natural gaits – walk, trot, and canter – which must be carefully cultivated and improved through disciplined work. With this training the horseman attempts, while working the horse under saddle, to maintain the balanced beauty and harmonious movement that is found in the 'untampered-with' horse.

When correctly implemented, dressage is above all a practical obedience training which prolongs the animal's usefulness and makes it a pleasure to ride. All forms of exercises, regardless of difficulty, including the High School airs above the ground, find their roots in the same movements in raw form in nature.

SYNONYMS for the word 'DRESSAGE'

- Work on the flat (this term used in jumping)
- English riding
- Training by the Natural Method
- Academic riding (encompasses the next two disciplines)
- High School riding (advanced work)
- The art of Classical riding (dressage in its ultimate form)

AN INTRODUCTION TO THE HORSES IN THIS BOOK

The horses that have been used to illustrate the text are all of the common 'back-yard' variety. The different breeds represented vary considerably in size, conformation, movement and temperament. Horses that have naturally good gaits, and which are naturally well balanced, offer the rider a great deal, and lessen the training problems substantially. For the rider who is capable, however, it is always interesting to work with equine material which is far from ideal, and carefully construct an end-product which is both pleasing to ride and to observe. When the basic motion of horses such as these can be improved, it stands as an irrefutable witness to the validity of effective practical gymnastics.

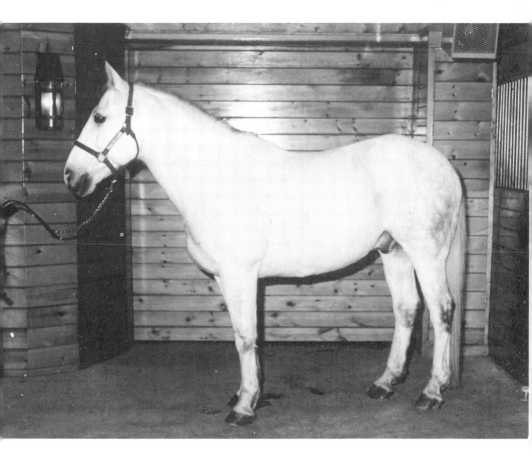

ATLANTIS

Grey gelding. Born 1966. Percheron-thoroughbred cross. 16.1 hh.
By nature he is a poor mover, his gaits are 'klunky'. Retraining this
fellow to become active, supple and obedient was like schooling a
heavy-weight wrestler to do ballet! He is a strong-minded, self-willed
horse. It proved to be a challenging task. Atlantis started his training
with the author at the age of 10. He was previously used as a family
'hack', and was occasionally hunted.

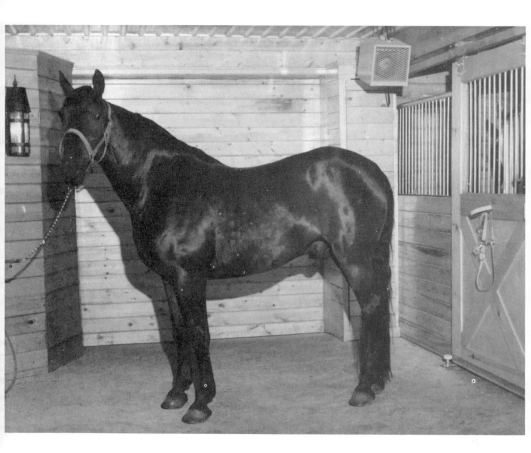

METEORITE

Dark brown gelding. Standardbred cross (?). Born (est.) 1963.
15.3 hh. Before being purchased by the author (1976) he had gone
the 'severe-bit route', and was quite thoroughly ruined. His mind
and body were knotted with tensions. It has taken over two years to
partially resolve the problems. This horse is represented in the book
to demonstrate the interesting and valuable examples of how tensions manifest themselves in the gaits. He is by far the most athletic
mover of these horses.

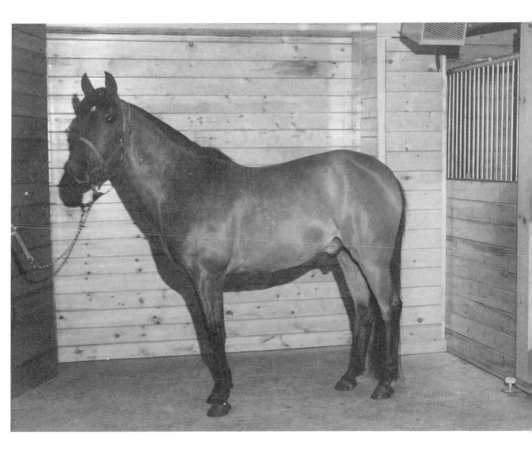

HAWTHORN'S BARGEL
(Barty)

Bay gelding. Born 1971. ¾ Arab–¼ Pony. 14.2 hh. He has a flat
'daisy-cutter' motion, with a dash of the choppy Pony gait added.
His jaw-throat-jowl area is tight and fleshy, therefore the 'forward
and down' exercises are demonstrated with him (which is an excellent exercise for horses with this particular conformation problem).
He is a very willing little chap!

The Author with Atlantis.

Part I

CHAPTER I

THE MENTAL PREPARATION OF THE RIDER

002
WHAT DOES THE RIDING TASK ENTAIL?

The horse already knows how to be a horse. The task of horseman-ship lies entirely with the rider. Through training, meaning the *conditioning* of the horse, the rider becomes able to guide the creature accurately through all the various movements which it can already perform naturally, and develop its athletic potential through discip-lined gymnastic work which is in harmony with its nature.

It is the primary duty of the horseman to be strictly a control centre, not a physical mover, shover, or pusher-puller of the animal. This state can only materialize when the rider, through consistent use of his aids, establishes a system of communication whereby the horse comes to understand what is wanted.

Besides becoming adept in the technical administration of the aids, the only physical responsibility to be mastered by the rider is, through balanced harmony, to become an entirely inseparable part of the horse, in no way disturbing or impeding the freedom of its body motion.

003
WHY THE MANY YEARS TO LEARN CORRECT RIDING?

Riding is like an intangible phantom. Its living, dynamic proportions cannot be measured or weighed. Though there are certain technicali-ties to be mastered, horsemanship is a task directed largely by elusive 'feels'. Two living creatures, each on entirely different physical and mental planes, attempt to become united. The unique character of each horse and personality of each rider, compounded with their own

3

individual physical variations and problems, comprise almost limitless combinations that must be dealt with in order to construct an end result in which the rider's mind does the thinking, and the horse's body does the doing.

While developing sufficient understanding and expertise we should adhere closely to the guidelines established by the great masters over the past four centuries. It is important to realize, however, that the application of any theory is usually dependent on a host of attendant conditions, and often only brings desired results when practised patiently and correctly over an extended period.

The inevitable difficulties of misinterpretation of theory can only be overcome gradually as each rider broadens his personal experience. In this way the commonly used words and concepts gradually flame into vivid colours of understanding; a knowledge which can only live in the act of doing.

004
AN ELABORATION OF PRACTICAL MENTAL ATTITUDES.

1) Each rider must travel every inch of the road personally. Nonetheless, theoretical study and taking lessons are vital directional aids, much like having a road map, that can assist the rider as he ventures into the maze of perplexing facets of horsemanship that lie on the road ahead.

2) We can best achieve good results by becoming constructively self-critical, cultivating a refined degree of mental self-control, and by being sufficiently mature to assess and compile the results of our performance realistically.

3) Through our instructors we are to learn how to *read the horse*. The horse's 'signs' are the key to our coming to understand its physical and psychological nature, and constitute our chief guideline for influencing it correctly. Preconception is a merciless, choking tyrant. There 'here' and 'now' during practice are the only truths that exist. Develop your feel, and let the horse be your guide from moment to moment.

4) It is entirely the duty of each rider to work diligently if high equestrian standards are to be attained. No matter how good the instructor or horses may be, unless the student is open-minded and receptive, only a relatively mediocre level will ever be attained.

5) The horse is in no way interested in our personal ambitions. Only when we have the correct combination of appropriate attitudes and an adequately clear administration of our aids, will the horse readily comply.

6) Horses are a far greater 'constant' than is commonly believed. It can be observed, time and time again, that when the rider is in a good mood and is feeling well, the horses invariably go well. Conversely, when the rider is in a poor mood, is burdened with worries, or lacks control over his emotions, the horses usually go badly. The horse will accurately mirror our favourable as well as undesirable attributes. (027, 059, 060–A & B)

7) It is the horseman's complete and sole responsibility, being the more intelligent, to find logical solutions to all problems within himself. There are always reasons . . . never excuses.

8) There is only one kind of mistake, that is, the *fundamental* mistake. Regardless of how advanced the exercise, if the performance is defective, one can directly trace that fault to a lack in the fundamental training of either the horse or the rider.

9) The chief motivator of our attitudes should be a love for the horses. When this theme encompasses all our intentions it fosters the humility and healthy learning attitude which aid us to persevere through the difficulties encountered on the road to discovering the horse.

10) We must learn to distinguish between a *judicious leadership* needed to guide the horse with firmness and persistence, and an *arrogant dictatorship* which is enforced through a thoughtless subjugation of the animal.

11) We should come to recognize our own limitations, thereby not demanding work from the horse that we ourselves are incapable of controlling. From this self-acceptance we will learn to gain enjoyment from small daily successes. It is far too seldom

appreciated what a mammoth task dressage riding assigns to us. Therefore we so frequently see riders over-facing their horses and themselves, and inadvertently having to resort to force, home-baked aids and trickery, in order to produced *supposed* results. Grade-schoolers do not learn advanced mathematics by the incessant repetition of University calculus problems. Yet precisely such ridiculous concepts are used in the training of both horses and riders. Without a solid basis for the work being asked, nothing but frustration in the rider, and contortion and unhappiness of the horses can result.

12) Contrary to popular belief, horses do not get bored with basic work. If the rider demands exact responses, paying close attention to detail and quality, neither horse nor rider will have time to get bored, rather, a true sense of accomplishment will be gained.

13) A subtle and insidious problem, and a point of some confusion, is that horses will readily conform to almost any riding method, provided its demands are relatively consistent. In other words, the horse will also yield to methods that do not regard its nature. This compliance occurs because the creature will do whatever is wanted in order to escape the wrath of man (should it disobey). However, false methods usually take their toll on the good creature: its useful life under saddle being truncated by early lameness caused by the unnatural, inefficient mode of travel which it has been forced to assume.

14) To work correctly entails dealing with an extremely delicate balance of natural values that can be all too easily ignored or overruled. The rider should therefore guard against stepping beyond the brink at which he becomes his own authority, and no longer listens to the horse for verification of the quality of his influences. Such a breech readily leads to the imposition of immodest demands at the expense of the horse and correctness of the work. This danger becomes more prevalent as the rider becomes more advanced.

15) Everyone has had to learn at some time, there is no shame in that, and no one can learn without making mistakes. Worth-

while things are seldom learned without experiencing some hardship. Suffering on both the horse's and rider's part is noble when the mistakes are honest, and a continuous attempt is made to improve, especially on one's virtues of patience and self-control.

16) The process of the rider's own learning often progresses at considerable expense to the horses. The animals experience great contradictions before the rider learns how to administer and coordinate his aids correctly. All of this the horses generally endure with great patience and good humour. A sympathy and compassion for the horses should therefore always rule, despite the rider's own frustrations and tribulations.

17) We can only become effective critics of our own work once we come to know what the necessary criterion is. *Understanding is the key to meaningful practice.* Much time is required, under close guidance, to learn to recognize all the fine nuances which differentiate the academic classical form of riding from artificial, trick or circus methods. Much can be learned, positively and negatively, from observing others ride, provided we remain objective in our criticism (have a truly studious attitude), and are empathetic with the person we are judging.

18) A close rapport between man and mount is the backbone of good horsemanship. The rider must respect the horse's physical strength, and, with the utmost of care, regard its nature. The horse must learn to respect and obey its intellectually superior master. The rider, however, must *earn* this respect through fair, consistent handling, discretely utilizing praise and correction.

19) Since the horse's reactions are many times faster than man's, it is only through conditioning by consistent work, and the rider's ability to prepare both himself and his horse, that an element of predictability gels between them ... the nucleus of a smooth performance.

20) If the horse becomes frightened and shies, or when it has suddenly been startled, our attitudes and reactions should be those which will maintain the horse's confidence in us. It would be a mistake to pull the horse about angrily, because this would

only confirm in the horse's mind that there was truly something to be frightened of. Instead, the rider should ignore that which is exciting or frightening the horse, and with a nonchalant air urge the horse to continue with the task at hand (if necessary using a reassuring voice). The rider must learn to become a strong, reliable and just leader . . . a kind, firm guiding force.

21) Punishment.

    (a)   When should one resort to punishment?

Generally, punishment should be a rarity. Considerable experience and understanding is required to determine whether punishment is actually warranted. The following points should certainly be taken into account: Were the aids correct and clear? Is the horse capable of executing the work being asked of it (over-facing)? Lastly, is it a clear case of disobedience?

    (b)   How can we punish fairly?

If it is determined that the horse must be punished, it should be done quickly and methodically, not out of ill-temperedness or lack of self-control, venting one's frustrations on the animal. Usually a smart whack with the stick, or an emphatic aid with the spur is more than adequate. Under certain circumstances, a stern voice aid can suffice to re-establish one's authority. If the horse is not punished immediately when the misdemeanour is committed it will not understand why it was punished.

    (c)   How much punishment is necessary?

The type and amount of punishment should be carefully suited to the character and sensitivity of the horse, and be proportionate to the severity of the infraction.

    (d)   The *come-back*. What to do after the correction has been made.

This last stage is essential to success but is a factor which is often neglected: reaffirming continued friendship and confidence. Once the correction has been made, do not linger on the matter, proceed immediately with a fresh start, as though nothing had happened, and reward the horse for even the slightest signs of cooperation. In this way the horse will readily learn that compliance with the rider's requests is rewarded with kindness and praise, but that disobedience is met with unpleasant reactions.

Note: Riders today seem to have become blunted to the sight, and concept, of people roughing-up their horses, and have come to consider this to be a necessary part of working the horse. For the knowledgeable horseman, however, it is a fail-safe sign, that if the horses frequently need to be 'beaten the heck out of' before they *apparently* submit and 'go well(!)', that the training is of the poorest order.

22) Ideal harmony is a product of trust. It cannot be dictated or forced out of any horse. Rather, it must be willed to come about by each participant, and can only be won by adequate, patient preparation and goodwill towards our four-legged partner.

23) We must always work with a clear purpose in mind: the accurate riding of school figures and a disciplined, meaningful choice of exercises. Aimless riding teaches neither us nor the horse anything.

24) The rider should end his work with an exercise that the horse can do easily. To finish on a happy note helps to prevent the carry over of negative attitudes, and a souring of the horse for future work.

25) In order to complete the mosaic of horsemanship, it is important that the background scene is conducive to the safety, comfort and peace of mind of the horses. Rough, indifferent handling causes the horses to become distrustful and frightened, or can make them into unpredictable rogues that acquire obnoxious habits of biting or kicking. Only if they are cared for with conscientious, quiet work and thoughtful handling while feeding, mucking-out, grooming and generally cleaning the stables,

will the horses settle down and be in a good frame of mind, and therefore be well prepared for their work in the manège.

REFLECTIONS I

- Armed with theory, practice becomes meaningful ... through practice, theory becomes fulfilled.
- Does the musician *work* the violin? Of course not! We too should always endeavour to '*play*' the horse, then it will work for us.
- A sizeable portion of the riding task lies in coming to grips with oneself.
- Every master has his horse.
- Rider's tact and feel cannot be taught ... it is for each individual to develop these within himself.
- Dressage is the fundamental obedience training ... for the rider!
- As we come to a deeper understanding of the horse's psyche, the more we discover how dependent we are on the horse's generosity.
- We should be particularly respectful of school horses, though they are often common creatures: it is upon their patient backs that we are lead to higher levels of horsemanship. There is always much to be learned from *any and every* horse.
- The horses are not bent on 'doing us in', we can only do ourselves in because of poor attitudes, or inexperience.
- Riding has to do with the nature of the horse, and not our whimsical preconceptions or pet theories.
- All that glitters is not classical riding.
- We should endeavour always to remain students of the horse; a learning process that is never finished.
- The line between very right, and very wrong, can be disconcertingly thin!
- For the true horseman no equestrian task is too menial.
- The challenge of dressage is not necessarily in having the best-moving horse, but rather to get every horse we ride to move as well as it possibly can.
- Patience ...

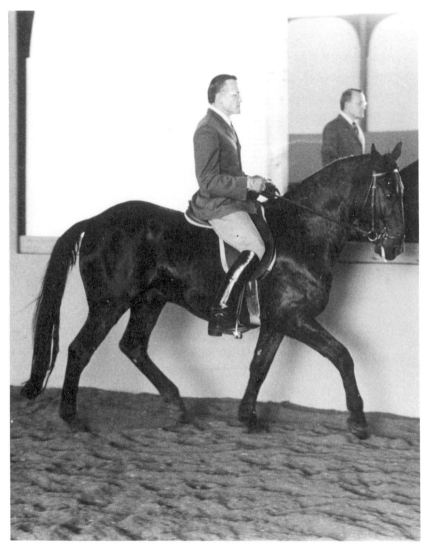

Meteorite. Working trot.

CHAPTER II

THE RIDER'S SEAT AND POSITION

Practice the fugue constantly, tenaciously, until you are tired of the subject and until your hand is so firm and so sure that you can bend the notes to your will . . . let us look back to the past: it will be a step forward.
GUISEPPE VERDI.

005
INTRODUCTION: THE PHYSICAL ATTITUDES

Within the physical attitudes we encompass the modes of the rider's seat and position. When considering the suitability of riders' basic 'raw materials' for the equestrian task, the physical attributes are secondary to the mental ones. Poor mental attitudes are devastating even if the rider enjoys good health, and perfect physical conformation for riding. Even though it may take many years of diligent work to gain the necessary independence and control of individual body parts, physical problems, outside of major bodily incapacitation, can all be brought under control and can somehow be compensated for.

Though correctness of the position is of great importance, one must not lose sight of the overriding need to remain thoroughly supple within this correctness. Involuntary tensions in the rider hamper the clarity and influence the aids, and restrict the freedom of movement in the horse's back, adversely affecting the purity of the gaits. The good position and seat should have an athletic poise, or bearing; a physical tone completely void of stiffness or contortion.

Despite this acknowledgement, it is important to realize and accept that an excellent seat and position is, with few exceptions, the fruit of hard work. Only after many years of stretching of stubborn, unwilling tendons and muscles of the hip joints and thighs, and the correcting of sloppy habits, such as slouched shoulders and collapsed chests, will the rider ultimately have produced a riding tool that can carry out the task of influencing the horse both effortlessly and correctly.

It is quite clear that during the years of 'forming' the seat and position, the rider may well be at times cramped and uncomfortable, and that subsequently the horses will not go well. Nonetheless, that is a price we should be willing to pay, realizing that as it becomes easier to maintain the suitable body posture, suppleness will gradually rule once more. To quote the words of Richard Wätjen, 'A fundamentally incorrect seat and position cannot be corrected through softness [ease]'. This certainly does not mean that the beginner can not have some good moments even very early on in their riding experience. Yet if we look only for ease and comfort before we have 'trained' our bodies, nothing but mediocrity and compromise can result.

It cannot be sufficiently strongly recommended to get this 'body forming' phase over with as early on as possible. Do stretching exercises off the horse daily, and make good posture a habit always, not just during riding! Furthermore, it should be realized that fairly constant attention must be spent on maintaining a good position to prevent regression.

006
THE FIVE MAJOR POSITION CORRECTIONS[1]

- Head up
- Stomach forward[2]
- Fists vertical
- Knees closed
- Heels down

The position corrections must be kept in as simple a form as possible, so that they are easily remembered during riding sessions.

---

[1] Egon von Neindorff.

[2] Lengthen the front line. Take care, however, not to hollow or stiffen the lower back!

14

Simplicity of the work load, that is, staying with one theme, is very important to acquiring any new physical attribute.

If, after having taken instruction, the rider has other corrections to make that pertain specifically to himself, then these should be added, in simple form, after the basic five. No seat or position will improve without the continuous mental repetition of these points, followed by the immediate physical correction.

007
THE SEAT

The seat comprises two major parts, 50 per cent is formed by the rider, the other 50 per cent is made up by the horse. However, both of these equal portions are entirely the responsibility of the rider. To be realistic, the sad fact needs to be stated that unless the rider is capable of causing his horse to carry him on an elastic, engaged back, a good seat cannot be cultivated. In other words, only the combined correctness of the rider's seat and position elastically balanced upon the supple, forward motion of the horse, can consumate a true unity. In order to cultivate a *good seat*, one must acquire a very thorough knowledge of the whole horse.

The rider's hips and seat, his thigh down to the knee, and his hand and forearm to the elbow, must become part of the horse entirely. The only physical parts of the rider which remain his own are, his head and upper body, and upper arm to the elbow, and his lower legs. The supple controlling links between these two categories are: *the lower back*, the lumbar vertebrae, acting as the chief controlling factor through which all aids are transferred to the horse, and *the supple elbows*, which act as a buffer to the horse's mouth.

008
THE CORRECT POSITION AND ATTITUDE OF THE SEAT

1) *The rider must sit straight down into the deepest part of the saddle,* with the seat bones having the attitude of being held into the front of the saddle.

2) *Sit mainly on the seat bones,* however, one should also be partially supported by the pelvic structure which lies between and in front of the two seat bones (the pubic crest.) These three points must be as though bolted down to the saddle at all times.

3) *Equal weight on both seat bones,* except when introducing the bend, riding on circles, bent lines, and two-track work, in which case the inside seat bone should have a *bit* more weight in it. (021, 028/1).

4) *Sit squarely in the saddle.* Do not collapse onto one hip.

5) *The hips must be held parallel to the horse's hips.* While riding on bent lines, or while bending the horse, the rider's inside hip is brought forward.

6) *The buttock muscles must be relaxed and opened,* this is in conjunction with well turned, relaxed hip joints and thighs. (019, and Chapter 9.)

009
THE SHOULDERS AND UPPER BODY

- The shoulders must be kept level. Common faults are:
  - (a)   One shoulder carried higher.
  - (b)   The inside shoulder held ahead of the outside one (skiing position).
- While riding on bent lines, the outside shoulder must be brought forward somewhat (shoulders parallel to the horse's shoulders). This is achieved by turning the whole upper body from the waist, and facing it towards the horse's inside ear.
- A helpful exercise to find the correct shoulder position is: Move the shoulders all the way forward and down . . . forward and up . . . up and back . . . back and down (an upside-down 'U').
- The rider's front line should be as long as possible. Think of making a capital 'D', or imagine that the upper body is a billowing sail, being filled by a breeze from behind.

16

010
THE UPPER LEG AND KNEE POSITION

Only a correct leg position and attitude will allow the rider to sit clearly on both seat bones. The legs should 'hang' down, like two wet towels. They gain the necessary substance (so that they do not dangle sloppily) by elastically stretching down through the heels. The thigh must be turned completely inward from the hip joint. To achieve this, it can be helpful to draw the thigh muscle out from underneath the femur by hand. This results not only in the correct opening of the buttock muscles, but also allows the knees to come in a holding contact with the saddle. Needing to have the knees closed should not be translated into a clamping-on or unnecessary gripping. The thigh muscle should lie relaxed on the saddle.

The upper leg to the knee, should point quite strongly to the ground; and when seen from the side, the hip and thigh should form a smooth, continuous line. The rider's leg should not be so straight, however, that he begins to sit on his thighs (fork or crotch seat). Conversely, if the knees are too high, the rider cannot effectively bring his weight into the seat bones and through to the ground (chair seat).

011
THE LOWER LEG AND FOOT POSITION

These are the main points:
  (a) When observing the rider from the side, the heel should be on the vertical line running through the centre of the rider's shoulder and hip.
       – leg aids are more effectively given from this position.
       – the rider is better able to find balance.
  (b) With the lower leg turned well inward, the rider should give the aids with the inside of the calf (imagine giving the aids with the shins). The foot should run almost parallel to the horse's sides. This attitude helps prevent the following problems:
       – sitting on the thighs.

- clamping-on with the lower leg.
- digging at the horse with the heels.

(c) Together with a relaxed ankle joint, the heel must be the lowest point of the rider. (This is the end result of correct sitting, when the whole leg comes to hang relaxed in the stirrup.)
- completes the total stretch from head to heel.
- helps draw the weight into the seat.
- the calf muscle is thereby lightly firmed, which helps to stabilize the lower leg.

(d) The lower leg should always be in a light holding contact with the horse's sides. It breathes with the horse. It should be as quiet as possible, though it may wave slightly with the motion of the horse's body. An exaggerated, incessant tapping is to be avoided.

012
THE ARMS

The arms must hang from relaxed, drawn back shoulders. The upper arms should lie lightly by the rider's sides. The lower arm and fist should be on a straight line from the bit to the elbow. We should imagine that the reins extend all the way to the elbow, so that the hand and forearm become an integral part of the leather. Both the wrist and elbow should always be supple and relaxed. The wrist may not be broken inward or outward. The back of the hand and the forearm should form a smooth continuous line.

Mistakes to watch out for:
- stiff outstretched arms, not enough bend in the elbow.
- broken wrists
- hands which are boring downward, or are held too high.
- stiffness in the wrist, elbow or shoulders.

013
THE FISTS

Both fists should be held at the same height. They must be held vertically, the thumbs uppermost. This is a very important requirement for it has been discovered that in this position the hand is the most sensitive and articulate; giving it the most liberty to move as directed by the horse's way of going. The hand must be perfectly quiet in relation to the horse's mouth. From this come the old saying, 'The hand stands still, but moves anyway'.[3] The hand's attitude should always be *alive*. This does not mean that it should fiddle about, but rather that it must be feeling; never stark, hard or unfriendly.

014
THE HEAD POSITION

The head must be held upright, since only in this mode can the weight of our entire upper body fall correctly into the seat. Keep in mind that a hanging head nullifies the driving ability of the seat, and lessens the effectiveness of all weight aids. Also to be avoided is the tipping of the top of the head inward or outward, especially during work on bent lines. One should, by and large, direct one's vision over the horse's head. Do not stick the chin out in front, keep it lightly drawn-in. 'Carry' the head quietly . . . *do not nod!*

015
THE CRITERIA FOR CORRECT RISING TROT

- The rider has a mobile, or dynamic, centre of balance which moves between the knee and seat.
- The inclination of the upper body is directly related to the centre of balance of the horse. If the horse is rushing or on the forehand, the upper body should be brought forward slightly to coincide with the horse's centre of balance; only then can the horse's

[3] Egon von Neindorff.

rhythm and balance be restored through driving. If the horse is in balance, and allows itself to be driven, then the upper body can be held closer to the vertical.

- The horse should move the rider; it shouldn't be necessary to stand up forcibly.
- The motion of the seat should be forward and back, the hips moving through the elbows; as opposed to an exaggerated raising of the seat up and out of the saddle. The rise should be as small as possible.
- Rise as the horse's outside front leg goes forward, and remember to switch diagonals when changing the rein, to exercise both sides of the horse equally. Sitting as the inside hind leg bears weight also assist in activating the horse.
- The *sit* is most important, it is the moment we can activate the horse. A non-sitting, hovering over the saddle is incorrect. However, do not drop or fall harshly onto the horse's back when coming to sit.
- Care must be taken to rise and sit squarely, to avoid a twisting or mincing motion of either the seat or shoulders.
- The knee and lower leg must be stationary. The knee acts as a pivot.
- The rider's weight should go clearly into his *relaxed* ankles at each stride, the heels showing a slight dip each time the rider rises.
- The hands are to be *absolutely motionless* without exception! This, however, does not mean rigid.

A FEW WORDS ABOUT SADDLES AND RIDING BREECHES

The use of friction materials, such as suede–covered breeches or saddles, does not help the rider find the real depth of seat required to achieve classical standards. Quite the contrary, in fact, such artificial aids of adhesion give the rider a false sense of closeness. They actually prevent the correct development of depth and harmony, which is based on balance, and an unrestricted fall-of-weight into the seat bones, and down through the heels towards the ground.

20

The cut of most 'off-the-shelf' riding breeches available today is far too tight. Though made of elastic material, these skin-tight breeches, or 'sausage casings', do not allow the thigh and buttock muscles to relax and form properly to the saddle. It is best to get breeches that have an inch or two of extra space in the thigh and seat, they should fit lightly and loosely in those areas. This will be found helpful especially for those who have heavy thighs. Learning to sit properly is a huge enough task that one doesn't need the added burden of being held back by restrictive clothing.

The trend towards saddles with 'deep seats' (!!) is another totally misleading phenomenon. *The rider's own seat must be deep*; meaning that it has found purest harmony with the horse. It is utter nonsense and self-deception to imagine that just because the saddle has a high pommel and cantle that therefore the rider will automatically be sitting more deeply. The finest saddles are those which *allow* the rider to sit where he should, yet in no way 'put the rider into any position'. The true position and seat are a result of years of work and correct experience, that, and that alone.

REFLECTIONS II

- The seat is the Alpha and Omega of riding (Egon von Neindorff).

- The hands must remain, strictly, each on its own side of the horse's neck.

- It is a serious fault to be sitting in the back of the saddle, being pushed along by the cantle. Leave plenty of saddle out behind the seat.

- If the rider's heels are continuously drawn up, the seat is fundamentally incorrect. (Such a seat inhibits the free forward motion of the horse.)

- Remember to let the horse do the work; the rider is only the control centre.

-- The seat cannot be cultivated as an isolated entity, its quality is directly related to the correctness of its influence on the horse.

- An artificial, superficial position without a good seat is worthless. A good seat, without an athletically good position, is impossible.

- It is essential that our breathing is always relaxed, even, and free.

- The hands are only ever as good as the seat.

- The rider can sit over the horse, on the horse, or *in* the horse. The last of these is the ultimate goal.

- All leg aids must be given from a closed knee (in light contact with the saddle flap).

- Too high a hand position robs the horse of the use of its back, and snubs-off the impulsion from the hindquarters.

- Use the 'razor' of your good seat wisely, and never against the horse. Like the surgeon's scalpel, it can either save or destroy with ease!

- Make your 'front line' long, but without hollowing the back.

– Hold your seat bones forward (have them leading you), but without leaning the upper body backward.

Atlantis. Shortened working canter right.

CHAPTER III

THE AIDS

To gain the fullest possible benefit from the contents of this chapter, it is essential that the reader does not falsely assume that there is a ready, cast-iron method to the administration of aids. Each moment of riding is unique. And so we must learn to use a truly living language when addressing the horse. It will be discovered that, within the basic parameters presented here *which are indispensible to correct aiding*, there exists considerable flexibility when applied in practice. One should therefore also not isolate any one of these factors since it is only through their combined harmonious use, 'The Symphony of Aids', that a competent guidance of the horse can evolve.

In any learning process the student must acquire suitable habits. This requires bringing many new and unfamiliar facets into the conscious mind before the desired *subconscious*, habitual behaviour can be formed. Naturally, the best results cannot be expected during this 'conscious effort' phase. Only once correct habits are firmly entrenched will the performance take on the essential aura of ease. All things, once learned properly, are easy – riding is no exception to this.

Though we need to work diligently, trying too hard brings only mental and physical tensions which result in blockage of the learning process. While learning to implement the elements put forth in the following pages, it is important to go ahead and JUST RIDE!, with a certain amount of free abandon (this can, of course, also be taken too far, to the point where one becomes careless). To 'just ride' means to work with a happy, positive attitude, and with a clear basic goal in mind: ride the horse forward on a specific school figure, and in the gait of your choice. Then, out of this stable set of circumstances, gradually introduce any new aspects, a few at a time, so as not to become so entangled in theory, that one can no longer 'see the riding for the aids'.

For a further elaboration on the technicalities and philosophy of the giving of aids, also refer to Chapter 8.

016
A DEFINITION OF THE AIDS

(a)   Aids are signals: the vocabulary of riding.
(b)   They must be brief and accurate: *a momentary* adjustment of the horse.
(c)   Be decisive, *get a result*. Aimless badgering only dulls horses.
(d)   When the result comes, *instantly stop* giving the aid; neutralize the hand, leg or seat.
(e)   *Contrast* is the strength and clarity of the aid!

017
PRINCIPLES IN THE GIVING OF AIDS

(a)   The driving aids (seat and legs) should predominate, by far exceeding the receiving or restraining aids of the hands.
(b)   Work the horse from back to front. Never pull the horse together by the reins.
(c)   Never use an active rein aid without a supporting *passive* leg and/or weight aid.
(d)   Use only *one* active aid at any one time; the other aids being passive and holding (supporting).
(e)   All aids must work in harmony towards *one single intention*. No contradictory aids.
(f)   Equal weight in both seat bones; except when giving specific aids, i.e. bending, changing direction, cantering-on etc., in which case the inside seat bone is made *momentarily* heavier.
(g)   Equal pressure in both legs; except when giving a sideways-yielding aid.
(h)   Equal pressure in both reins; except when giving a bending or straightening aid. (True equality in the reins is achieved via a supple, compliant horse.)

Split second, correct timing in giving aids or praise and correction, and also the suitable length of duration of an aid, is of the utmost importance to achieving successful reactions from the horse.

The aids should not be a monologue, blindly thundering from the rider. One must become subject to, and allow oneself to the directed by, the horse: its degree of training, temperament, and sensitivity, and also by the varying circumstances as they present themselves each day or from moment to moment.

An indispensible factor to improved riding lies in cultivating one's sensitivity. *Only when we can feel a result from our aids will the horse begin to react to them consistently*. In the conscious use of an aid, and in the awareness of the reaction it has elicited from the horse, lies the difference between true aids and accidental movements.

The quality of the aids, or lack of same, is in direct relation to the skill and experience of the rider. The less experienced rider still needs to use relatively coarse, obvious aids. The advanced rider can tune a horse so finely that response is attained from mere suggestions.

018
THE BASIC FUNCTIONS OF THE NATURAL TOOLS IN THE GIVING OF AIDS

The prime function of the natural riding tools, the seat, hands and legs, is to *passively* contain, form, hold, and guide the horse. From this neutral, passive state the basic tools perform specific MAIN functions which are given below.

THE SEAT: All aids find their basis in, or act through the seat to the horse's back (021).

– UNILATERAL AIDS, the rein and leg on the same side, act as containing aids. (032, framing the horse.)

– DIAGONAL AIDS, for example; the inside leg[1] and outside rein, influence the horse in active and passive diagonal pairs. They are used to affect the bend, or straightness of the horse, or to establish the two-track positions. A description follows.

THE ACTIVE DIAGONAL PAIR:[2]

INSIDE LEG:	gives the active driving aid; it also acts like a post around which the horse is bent.
OUTSIDE REIN:	controls the pace, the rhythm, and affects the balance and carriage. It limits the amount of bend. It is the chief guiding rein. (052, the half-halt.)

The active aid is given by nudging or vibrating within the application of pressure.

THE PASSIVE DIAGONAL PAIR:

OUTSIDE LEG[3]:	holds the quarters from swinging out; as a driving leg, has the same pressure as the inside leg but remains passive (022).

[1] How do we know which is the inside? This is determined by the rider. Regardless of on which hand one rides in the school, that direction in which the rider wishes to bend the horse will be the inside.

[2] The requirement of only one active aid at any one time still applies. THESE TOOLS ARE ONLY TO BE ACTIVE WHEN NECESSARY! Once the desired reaction has been achieved from the horse, they should instantly return to their home base of neutrality.

[3] When the leg is in the normal position (011, a) it acts on the horse as a driving aid. If the leg is held back from this position by 4"–5", it acts as a containing aid when passive, and a sideways-yielding aid when used actively and with more pressure.

28

INSIDE REIN: supports the bending
                 aids, that's all! Do not pull
                 back! (028–B)
The passive aid comprises the application of a
steady, uniform, elastic pressure.

WHAT FUNCTION DOES THE HAND PLAY?

In its function as regulator of the pace, the hand can be compared to
the nozzle on the end of a garden hose. When the rider does not take
up the contact (loose rein), it would be the same as completely
removing the nozzle from the hose; the water, not being restricted,
just falls out. When the contact is taken up, the nozzle now starts to
play the role of accurately controlling the amount of water leaving the
hose. When the nozzle is shut, the water (horse) stops. When the
nozzle opens more or less, and depending on the amount of pressure
generated by the pump (driving aids), the result is either a fine,
powerful mist (collected work, Piaffe), or a strong, forceful jet of
water (extended trot).

If there is no pressure control on the pump (ruthless, insensitive
use of the driving aids), and should the nozzle be shut (a hard,
resisting hand), the hose would rupture somewhere along its length
(the horse first becomes excited, then if pressure isn't released, the
horse would *explode* by rearing, bucking or kicking out behind, or
becoming evasively crooked, in order to relieve the overload of
pressure in its body. The more mild manifestations of this would be:
tensions, stiffness, resistance, rushing, constrained motion, and
choppy gaits).

The nozzle is only of value as a *passive* control when the water
pump operates properly. Similarly, the hand only functions correctly when the driving aids supply it with sufficient forward energy.

THE VOICE: Horses react quite readily to the voice.
                 This can be used advantageously
                 especially during training. When sounds
                 are calm and soothing they have a relax-

	ing, confiding effect. If, however, the voice is stern or sharp it can be used as a mild form of punishment.
THE SPURS AND WHIP:	These are considered artificial aids, and are only used to sharpen the horse's response to the natural aids (024, 064).

019

THE CORRECT ATTITUDE AND DRIVING INFLUENCE FROM THE SEAT

It cannot be sufficiently strongly emphasized that the rider learns to command a good position, and master a precise control over his lower back and hips, in order to be able to concentrate his weight correctly into the seat bones.

The essence of the driving seat is constituted in a sitting more deeply into the motion of the horse. It is principally a weight aid which can be given with greater or lesser intensity. *The optimum the seat can do is to be absolutely quiet in relation to the horse's back.*

THE THREE MAIN ATTITUDES OF THE SEAT

1) The 'following', neutral seat; wholly non-influential.
2) The 'maintaining' seat, attained through 'pelvic tilt' which results in the seat bones (pubic crest) being held more or less emphatically forward. The seat must continue to flow with the motion.
3) 'Bracing the back', which is central to the driving influences, also provides the reins with a base for support or resistance, which is transferred via the seat to the horse's back. Bracing is wholly contained within the 'stretching the front line', and 'pelvic tilt' attitudes. Bracing varies in duration and intensity as needed. Even during 'bracing', the seat should always remain elastic and harmonious on the horse's back, never cramped or stiff. (For details see Chapter 9, pages 142–144.)

THE POINTS OF OPTIMUM DRIVING INFLUENCE FROM THE SEAT:

1) A well stretched position from head to heel.
2) A vertical, quiet upper body. Head held up.
3) A supple lower back, neither hollowed nor rounded.
4) Seat bones held more or less emphatically and elastically forward (pelvic tilt).
5) Bracing the back, more or less as needed.

With this attitude the rider *increases* his weight in the seat, and the centre of balance falls toward the back of the seat bones. The optimum driving influence comes from the combined use of the seat with coinciding pressure from both legs. Though it is hard to conceptualize without having experienced it, driving from the seat is a *passive* activity; a deep emphasizing of the rhythm, such as one might do while dancing, yet without in any way appearing 'busy'.

POINTS OF THE NON-DRIVING ATTITUDE OF THE SEAT:

1) Upper body leaning forward, and/or
2) completely limp, relaxed lower back, and/or
3) lower back hollowed *deliberately*.
4) The forward seat (jumping posture), the rider's seat is taken completely out of the saddle.

With this attitude the seat is made *lighter*; the rider's centre of balance falls towards the front of the seat bones.
(Note: *For a more detailed elaboration on the functions, attitudes, and influences of the seat, see Chapter 9.*)

020
THE INCORRECT ATTITUDES AND DRIVING INFLUENCES OF THE SEAT AND POSITION

- Head nodding, looking down.
- Shoulders heaving, rounded.
- Back hunched; collapsed upper body.
- Upper body leaning forward or backward.
- Much pelvic movement; loose doughy seat, stomach flopping.
- Unquiet knees; loose or rolling thighs.
- Sitting mainly on crotch, thighs, or seat muscles.
- Exaggerated tapping with lower legs; heels drawn up.
- Any rigidity, stiffness, or tensions. These result in the seat bouncing in the saddle, and unquiet hands that flap up and down at each trot and canter stride.
- It is incorrect to think of the driving influence from the seat to be an active pushing (pumping) motion on the saddle.

021
WHAT IS A WEIGHT AID?

The weight aid is constituted in the rider's ability to determine precisely where his weight (centre of balance) falls into his seat bones. Firstly, when the weight falls toward the front or back of both seat bones equally, a *bilateral weight aid*, it influences the horse as a driving aid (more or less). Secondly, by increasing the weight in only one of the seat bones, a *unilateral weight aid*, it influences the horse as a bending or steering aid (028–A, 1).

These weight aids are generally very subtle, and only become effective once the rider has learned to sit quietly, and cause his centre of balance to coincide with the horse's centre of balance: that is, putting the horse correctly *on the aids* (037, 038).

THE TIMING OF THE DRIVING AID FROM THE LEGS

The influences which can be achieved by the driving aid are heavily dependent on timing. If we wish to get a *stronger, forward-surging response* at the trot, the driving aid should be given during the last half of the weight-bearing phase (and up to the moment of thrusting off). If we wish to achieve a *greater action* of the horse's legs, and/or a *loftier gait*, such as is desirable for Passage, for example, the best timing comes exactly at the moment the hoof is thrusting off, and as it begins to rise off the ground. At the canter the driving aid is given during the moment of suspension. At the walk the driving aid is given as each hind leg comes off the ground and during the time when it swings forward and under the rider's seat. Unless the driving aid is given at the correct time, and in rhythm with the gait, it can actually inhibit the fluidity of the horse's movements.

At the walk:	Both of the rider's legs activate the corresponding hind leg of the horse *actively*. It is an alternating left/right leg aid.
At the trot and canter:	The rider's inside leg gives the aid *actively*; the outside leg gives the same pressure but remains passive. The importance of this equal but passive driving with the outside leg cannot be over-emphasized, it is commonly neglected. In exceptional cases, when a strong driving aid is needed, both legs may drive actively. Always remember to consider the appropriate driving attitude from the seat while activating the horse.

IMPORTANT FACTORS ABOUT ACTIVATING THE HORSE

In the ability to activate lies one of the most important fundamental requirements of the riding task. Only when the rider can, 1) initiate and control the true forward urge, 2) allow it to occur by an appropriate hand attitude, and 3) flow forward (harmonize) with the horse's movements, will he actually control the horse correctly. When the horse goes truly forward, a multitude of evasions and problems are automatically eradicated (044). Though it is true that tensions and resistances can be 'driven out the front', this has nothing to do with ruthlessly chasing the horse forward, helter-skelter, without regard for rhythm or suppleness. The following points give guidance.

1) Avoid driving the horse more than it can accept, or tensions will be caused in its back.
2) As is commonly known, true work does not begin until the horse becomes lazy. The horse must let itself be driven. The rider must not mistake nervous or excited energy for true forward impulse. The horse must first be mentally at ease (029, 2) and physically relaxed, and be in a correct rhythm before it can be asked for more stepping from behind.
3) If the rider forces the horse forward despite the animal's hard, hollow back, he will only cause the horse to resist more and find evasions in crookedness, rushing, or a constrained forward motion.
4) The activating aids should not degenerate into a physical moving of the horse. It should be an effortless task to send the horse on, once it is put correctly on the aids. The rider should have a clear mental intention while activating: think of filling a beach balloon under the saddle, and attaining a *longer* stride and/or a *rounder* motion while remaining in the same rhythm (052, the half-halt). Remember to *allow* the horse to go forward through the light hands, and to flow harmoniously with the motion at all times.

INDICATIONS OF THE HORSE'S ACCEPTANCE OR REJECTION OF THE AIDS

A highly detailed outline of points which are a guideline for how much activating is suitable for the horse's state of suppleness, balance, and level of training, can be found in sections 059 and 060–A & B. These are also good indicators for setting limitations on the level and complexity of exercises; when and for how long to do sitting trot (young horses); and what degree of collection is acceptable at any given state of training.

If any of the 'positive' aspects fall by the wayside, and any of the 'negative' signs show their ugly head, the rider should lessen the demands on the horse: simplify the exercises or school figures; ride freer gaits; and with young horses go back to rising trot.

025
TUNING THE HORSE TO AIDS FROM THE SEAT AND LEGS

1) The correct aid from the seat and legs has been given . . . the horse responds sluggishly.
2) Repeat the aid from seat and leg, and *simultaneously* reinforce the aid with the use of stick or spur(s).
3) The next time the aid needs to be given, do so with the seat and legs alone, checking whether or not the horse has actually become more responsive to the natural aids.
4) The moment the horse responds: *neutralize*, and praise it with voice or a pat on the neck.
5) This sequence is to be repeated until the horse responds willingly, without the support of the artificial aids.

By and large, the stick should be used for supporting the driving aids, and the spurs for enforcing the sideways-yielding aids. However, their use can be interchanged if necessary.

Furthermore, it is essential to realize that the leg/stick are the only means by which the rider can tune the horse to the subtle influences from the seat which should ultimately be the major communicator of all the rider's intentions to the horse.

026

THE QUALITY OF THE REIN CONTACT

(a)   Soft and light.
(b)   Elastic at all times.
(c)   Even though the contact may need to become heavier for brief moments, when offering the horse resistance, it may never become hard.

The rein aids must be transmitted through a continuous contact, which is to be *unconditionally reliable*, never from a slack, flapping 'wash line'.

The softness, elasticity and sensitivity of the *living contact* originates from a balanced seat and an entirely independent upper body, and is transmitted through supple, relaxed shoulders, elbows and wrists to the friendly hands; such as a pleasant handshake between people. The limp, opened hand that holds the reins towards the fingertips is to be avoided; it is a false notion of softness, and furthermore, leads to continuous slipping of the reins.

027

THE QUALITY, QUANTITY AND INTONATION OF THE AIDS

Anyone can sit on a horse . . . pull on the reins . . . squeeze with the legs . . . or hit the horse with a whip. This in itself, however, obviously doesn't make one a good or effective rider.

The main task in all the years of learning how to administer correct aids is encompassed in the discovering of *how much*. Not only must one dispense exactly the appropriate amount, but the quality and texture of each aid also plays a decisive role.

Horses have an uncanny talent for perceiving the most subtle

36

nuances that are often transmitted subconsciously by the rider. If, therefore, the horseman learns to channel these mental intentions deliberately, it facilitates a completely new horizon of communication with the animal.

In the telling of jokes lies an example of the intonation which can colour the aids. The words alone, however clever they might be, play only a relatively small part in the presentation of wit. When the feeling for suitable expression, gesture and timing is lacking, the joke often falls flat. Similarly with the giving of aids, one can either fail or succeed, depending frequently only on this talent for appropriate timing and inflection; this embodies the full spectrum of equestrian tact.

028–A
THE SEQUENCE OF CHANGING POSITION AND AIDS WHEN CHANGING THE REIN

Though the position change is a rapid sequence, one should follow this order. These points apply any time the horse is being bent.

1) CHANGE THE SEAT: The new inside seat bone must be slightly ahead of the outside one, and with a bit more weight in it. This extra weight must also flow down through the deeper inside knee, and into the stirrup and heel.

2) CHANGE THE DRIVING LEG: The horse must be bent around the new inside leg which acts like a post. It also gives the active driving aid. As the legs are changed, slide them along the horse's sides, do not take them off. Always make a clear distinction when changing the leg positions: the inside leg at the normal position near the girth, and the outside leg held well back (4″–5″), passively supporting the quarters from swinging out.

3) CHANGE THE BENDING REIN AIDS: These will only be
obeyed when the seat and leg aids have
been correct. The bending rein aids
should always be given in an elastic, *asking*
manner.

028–B
ESSENTIAL POINTS FOR CORRECT BENDING

- Implement all bending influences with a predominating *forward*
intention. Always keep the gaits pure, correct, and fluid.
- Keep the horse tracking straight (029, 3, single-track work).
- Increase the weight of the inside seat bone. This is critical!!
- Adjust the seat and legs (028–A).
- *Passively*, and elastically, resist on the inside rein.
- Play out the outside rein *slightly* without losing the contact.
- Maintain an even rhythm and correct tempo, preventing the horse
from running away from the bending influence (half-halt).
- Be sure the horse's ears remain on the same level. It is a common
error for the nose to tip inward and for the horse's outside ear to
drop down during incorrect bending because of a dominant inside
rein, tensions, or a lack of forward energy (032, e).
- If the horse resists, the rider may introduce an active kneading
pressure at the girth with the inside leg, directed towards the
outside rein and shoulder. Besides underscoring the impulsion,
this helps to bend the horse through its whole body, and prevents
the horse from cutting-in.
- If necessary, as a last resort, *this truly must be seen as an exception*,
the inside hand may give small active *feels* on the rein (in order to
keep the rein 'alive' while WAITING for the horse to decide to
soften). Be sure to avoid pulling back under any circumstances.
RIDE FORWARD!
- When the horse does yield to the bend, the rider too must instantly
equalize the pressure of both reins (lighten the inside rein, and
become totally neutral *in that bent state*).
- Only if the horse should voluntarily try to straighten, against the

rider's wishes, or if the rider expressly wants to alter the bend, should any further bending aids be given.

– Do not overbend the horse's neck – that is, beyond seeing a glimpse of the inside eye and nostril rim.

– Besides bending the horse through its body, most of the bend in the neck should take place towards its end (behind the ears especially) and not at its base.

– Only when the horse has yielded to the inside rein can the outside rein be judiciously brought into play to help further the bend more clearly through the horse's body.

Ideally, through suitable training, all bending should be attained through a subtle, and wholly passive, lateral forming of the horse. Remember that the most important principle of any bending is that the horse yields to the inside rein by stretching the *outside* of its body. Furthermore, at the risk of stating the obvious, it is imperative to stress that the horse must actually *yield* to the bending aids. The common problem being that the horse may well be bent but that it has not *softened* – yielded willingly – in which case it will have merely formed a concrete arc.

HOW DOES THE DISEASE 'INSIDE-REIN-ITIS' MANIFEST ITSELF?

Through the *incorrect*, direct use of the inside rein the rider attempts to:

– pull the horse onto circles with it
– pull the horse through corners with it
– pull the horse into shoulder-in with it
– do turns on the haunches with it
– make the horse leg-yield with it
– generally keep the horse from cutting-in by pressing the inside rein against the neck (instead of using the inside leg).
– bend the horse solely with the inside rein without

the use of the other, more important elements (028–B).

Avoid, like death itself, any of the above misuses of the inside rein! The rider must learn to guide the horse mainly with the seat and legs. In the above mentioned instances, the reins should play largely a *framing* role. (032, framing the horse.)

REFLECTIONS III

- Only a truly supple, relaxed horse can correctly obey a rein aid.

- Our reactions must be lightening-quick, but our attitude towards the horse should be as though we had all the time in the world. It is a calmness that seems at odds with the speed of reaction.

- Always prepare yourself mentally and physically before asking your horse for anything.

- It must be the rider's chief aim to cause the horse to respond to ever lighter aids.

- It must be considered a serious fault to ride the horse with the whip or spurs only, without first having given the aid properly with the seat and legs.

- When animating remember: 'DRIVE, ALLOW, GO WITH . . .'.

- Never ambush or surprise your horse with any aid.

- The rein and leg of the rider on one side affects directly the corresponding hind leg of the horse.

- The energy which is generated by the legs in *pounds* . . . should be received in the hand in *ounces*.

- No aids will affect the horse more adversely than harsh, unfeeling rein aids.

- Only when the rider becomes quiet will the horse be able to hear the whispers of the finer aids.

- The hands must give the hind legs space to step, they should have a yielding attitude towards the horse's mouth. This does *not* mean to give the reins away measurably; it is in the truest sense of the word only an *attitude of yielding* or allowing.

- We must have a clear mental intention while giving any aid, or the riding will quickly degenerate into strictly a physical task.

Barty. 'Forward and down' at the working trot.

CHAPTER IV

WORKING THE HORSE

029
THE PRINCIPLES OF RIDING

The three cardinal principles of riding are: Forward, Calm, and Straight.

1) FORWARD: –   The supple, balanced horse going actively in a correct, even rhythm. An unconstrained, fluid motion, neither rushing nor lazy. It is the basis on which all honest work is built.

            –   Rushing means, the horse is going in too fast a rhythm; chasing, unbalanced, on forehand, tense.

            –   Lazy means, the horse may well be in the correct rhythm but isn't active from behind; a dull, expressionless, unbalanced motion,

2) CALM: –   The horse is calm when it is mentally at ease, in a co-operative, unagitated state of mind, whereby it allows its energies to be usefully directed by the rider. It does not mean that the horse is a dullard.

            –   The horse is not calm when:

               (a) Adversely affected by outside stimuli; this includes the rider.

               (b) 'High' from being in the stall for an extended period. Overfeeding of grain combined with insufficient work.

(c) When it has a nervous temperament.

3) STRAIGHT: – Straight work is referred to as *work on a single track*.

– A horse is straight when its hind feet travel in the same path as its front feet.

– Within the above requirement, the horse's spine and neck must also be bent exactly on the form of the line or figure being ridden.

– True straightness further requires that the horse is correctly on the aids; that through suppleness and activity, the horse accepts both sides of the bit equally: a genuine state of self-carriage in which both the lateral and longitudinal pairs of legs are equally loaded, balanced.

– The volte is the smallest curved line on which the horse is able to form its body (about 16 to 18 feet in diameter). It is therefore the natural limit of single-track work. If the rider wishes to make smaller turns, then correct two-track work must be used, culminating in turns on the haunches.

030

THE SIX MAJOR GUIDELINES FOR CORRECT RIDING AND TRAINING

– Rhythm
– Relaxation
– Contact
– Straightness
– Impulsion
– Collection

44

It must be noted that these are individual stages of riding or training. One must achieve each single requirement before the next step can be attained. There must be a boringly even, correct *rhythm* before *relaxation* (or unconstraint, or the apparent onset of 'laziness') will be reached, (023); only a relaxed horse will profitably allow itself to be driven, resulting in a correct *contact*, which the horse searches for and takes up; once the horse reaches for the bit *straightness* can start to be addressed and attained; only a straight horse (029, 1) can begin to develop *impulsion*, and improve in its suppleness which, after the appropriate length of training, can be furthered to a true *collection*.

031
FUNDAMENTAL AIMS IN TRAINING THE HORSE

- Initial handling and longeing sessions to acquaint the youngster with the bridle, saddle, and tack; these are the first simple obedience lessons.
- The horse must become accustomed to the carrying and balancing of the rider's weight on a supple, elastic back.
- The horse must learn to obey the rider's wishes – control, responsiveness, accuracy in riding of school figures and execution of exercises. If the horse is not over-faced, obedience poses few problems, and only minimal time needs to be spent exclusively on it. *Every aid is a small obedience lesson.*
- Gymnastic training; the building of muscle structure, tendons, heart and lungs for strength and endurance, and to fully develop the balance and athletic qualities of the horse. The greatest skill, experience, and time in training are spent on this work.
- Gradually and systematically the more advanced exercises are introduced, as the horse becomes able to cope with the work, without causing either physical or psychological damage.

When the horse is carefully steeped in a consistent routine, handled with firm kindness and respect, the animal becomes mentally mature and mellowed ... a willing and generous worker, confident in mankind.

032

FRAMING THE HORSE

- In order to gain precise control, the rider must *frame* the horse.
- To frame means to *contain* the horse within the clear perimeter of the rider's natural tools: the legs, hands, and seat (018).
- The rider's legs (containing the body and quarters) and reins (containing the neck and shoulders) must form a channel, like two river banks, through which the horse is allowed to flow forward. The left rein and leg contain the left side, the right rein and leg contain the right side.
- *Both legs and both reins must have a continuous contact with the horse.*

If the contact of any one of these is lacking, then the horse is no longer framed, and it gives the horse a hole through which it can escape. Crookedness may result, and also a poor control over the rhythm, activity and balance. It is particularly essential that both reins stabilize the base of the neck onto the withers and shoulders, quietly and passively preventing any snakiness of the neck at this location.

Even if the rider has a contact with both reins and legs, there are more subtle ways in which the animal is not framed. These are some of the common evasions:

(a) Opening or crossing the jaw. (Can be prevented by appropriate adjustment of the noseband [not too tight]; riding with a light hand, while sending the horse forward.)

(b) Drawing-up or sticking-out of the tongue. (The result of riding with hard, dominating, or dead hands. Forced riding.)

(c) The base of horse's neck is bent laterally, more than the curve of the line being ridden. (This prevails when the horse is not bent evenly throughout its body. The neck is over-bent, being broken sideways just ahead of the withers.) The horse can escape the rider by falling against the outside shoulder, or running-out. (Can be prevented by straightening the horse's neck, and using the outside rein and leg more clearly as a containing wall.)

(d) The horse's neck is broken or kinked, horizontally, at the third vertebra behind the poll. The neck and spinal column are no longer a continuous entity, whereby the basic requirement for putting the horse correctly on the bit no longer exists: the forehand and hindquarters are not united, and the location of the horse's head is not relevant to its way of going. It is therefore a very serious fault, since the horse has effectively come behind the bit. This is a result of forced riding, the horse's head has been pulled down without regard for its natural balance. (Can be corrected by bold forward riding [maintain the rhythm], and the forward and downward exercise, 039.)

(e) The horse tipping its head sideways, or warping its neck. The ears are no longer on the same level. Can be a result of forced riding; a lack of forward urge; a predominant inside rein, or unequal pressure in the reins; the horse is bottled-up and tense. Besides riding the horse forward, this can be corrected by driving more with the leg on the side of the horse's higher ear, while *thinking* of the rein on the side of the lowered ear.

033
THE FRAMING FUNCTION OF THE SEAT

By sitting down correctly the rider is able to hold the horse *in front* of the seat and leg. This directly influences the presence of the hindquarters underneath the seat, and prevents the horse from going in a broken-apart manner. *He who has control of the hind foot of the horse, controls the whole horse* (008, 019). Important, see Chapter 9.

034
THE CRITERIA FOR THE CORRECT HEAD POSITION OF THE HORSE

1) Poll is the highest point of the whole horse.

2) Nose slightly ahead of, or on the vertical line.
3) Ears on the same level.

035
COMPLETION OF THE CIRCUIT

The circuit can only be complete if both horse and rider are entirely void of tensions and resistance. Only through suppleness can the horse's hindquarters react correctly to the driving aids and begin to carry more weight (044). This entails the correct use of the horse's 'muscle ring', i.e., the back, stomach, and neck muscles are harmoniously and actively in play.

The rider, being the motivator of the action, causes the horse to step actively through its back. The impulse travels through the horse's spinal column, neck, poll, and jaw to the bit, then through the reins into the rider's fists, elbows, shoulders and the rider's spine, which reacts directly, via the seat bones, upon the horse's back once more. This completion of the circuit (when the rider's leg and seat influences arrive in his hands via the supple horse: *leg in hand*) is the basis for all correct work.

036
'ON THE AIDS' – VERSUS – 'COLLECTION'

The term 'collection' is quite often carelessly used to mean: 'Gather your horse up, put it together'. (In other words, put the horse 'on the aids'.) Here is a brief description of both concepts.

A horse must be *put on the aids*, which is a 'putting together by suppling and balancing'. As a consequence the horse finds the correct head position. It is the foundation for all correct work. A horse which is 'on the aids' is thereby prepared to execute the three gaits from *extreme extensions* to the highest degree of collection (depending on its individual level of training).

Collection itself, however, is a state attained only after many years of systematic, gymnastic work, and manifests itself in a shorter, higher, rounder stride, which has been achieved solely through forward impulse. The horse's motion must remain fluid, and must always continue to show the correct sequence of footfall in all gaits (045, 047, 048). True collection is marked by a clear lowering of the croup, because of the deeply bent and engaged haunches that carry more weight. This depth of bending is the result of the elasticity of the three major joints: hip, stifle, and hock; this cannot be achieved without suppleness throughout the whole horse.

037
WHAT DOES 'ON THE AIDS' MEAN?

The horse which is being ridden on the loose rein is like a bow which has not yet been strung, one cannot quickly or effectively shoot arrows with it. When the horse is put 'on the aids', its body becomes spanned like a compressed spring – the strung bow. This compression occurs when the horse obeys the activating aids and commences to step impulsively through its back, and begins to stretch its whole body for the bit. As it finds resistance at the bit (because the rider doesn't yield with the reins), the horse's neck rises *up* off the withers, and the forward energy is converted into a carrying energy (balance). This converting can occur only if the horse willingly yields at the poll (this should in no way be forced). From this series of events the hindquarters become more loaded, and the centre of balance moves back, beneath the rider's seat. The horse subsequently also finds a suitable, natural head position that is in harmony with its way of going. When this state can be maintained in all three gaits and through all simple school figures, and transitions, then the horse can be considered to be well 'on the aids'.

It is particularly through the unification of the horse's and rider's centres of balance, the result of a correct 'putting on the aids', that the horse becomes liberated, and enables it to respond easily and instantly to the rider's wishes. Only once this coinciding of centres of balance materializes, do the weight aids find their true impact.

When the young horse is put on the aids, the neck rises very gently up off the withers, and the nose is still well in front of the vertical. With more advanced horses, which have improved in their balance, suppleness and activity, the neck rises more markedly up from the withers, and the nose comes closer to the vertical. The correct head position (034) is only of value when it is the *end result* of the horse balancing itself by stepping actively through its back.

The head and neck position of the horse should be seen as a barometer, indicating the state of the horse's way of going. As long as the rider works the horse in accordance with correct principles, this barometer is an accurate guide. If, however, false methods are used (placing the head and neck artificially) the barometer shows a false reading: it indicates that the weather is 85 degrees and sunny, when in actual fact, it might well be 40 below zero with a blizzard going on; this would clearly be a fool's paradise!

038
HOW IS THE HORSE PUT 'ON THE AIDS'?

It is essential that the rider learns to put the horse 'on the aids' quickly and effectively. It is the fundamental state from which all work commences. To put the horse on the aids the rider must cause it to respond to the following series of aids:

- the forward driving aids
- the bending aids
- the sideways yielding aids from the legs.

As a result of response to the above three categories of aids, the horse will consequently begin to accept the receiving/restraining aids from the reins. Remember, the reins play largely a passive, receiving role. It is also important to note that the correct lateral bend, and the longitudinal yielding of the horse in its back/neck/poll occur wholly in conjunction with one another, neither is complete without the other. The driving and receiving influences must work in harmony to achieve the 'on the aids' state.

- The horse should be put on the aids at the walk (young horses excepted, 045), by riding voltes and bent lines with frequent changes of rein (057).

Barty. 'Forward and down' at the working canter left.

- The horse must be framed (031).
- The rider must offer the horse an even, elastic contact.
- It is essential to maintain an absolutely even, correct rhythm, to cause the horse to relax its back; the half-halt plays an important role (052). *Use a filtering hand, not a blocking one.*
- While putting the horse 'on the aids', the rider must, as needed, continuously *lure* impulsive forward stepping from the hind-quarters, activating the horse into both reins. (This active driving can be lessened once the horse comes on the aids, and has found self-carriage.)

51

Only through tactfulness and sensitivity can a favourable response be expected from the horse. In projecting a quieting influence, the rider gains the creature's confidence, and contributes to the general suppleness and relaxation. (This does not mean physical laxity!)

In the appropriate ratio between the activating aids from the seat and legs, and the suitable restraining attitudes of the hands, lies the key to control over the increased loading of the hindquarters, and therefore the balance of the horse. This balanced state must be born out of the forward impulse of the three gaits; referred to as *relative erection* of the head and neck. It can only be achieved and maintained through the predominant (this does not mean *continuous*!) use of the driving aids.

If the horses's head position has been artificially achieved through the direct, active use of the hand (the backward-working, predominant hand) which is referred to as *active erection* of the head and neck, the resulting exterior appearance of the horse will have no correlation to either the impulsion, balance, or the willing compliance of the horse. (The German riding master, Julius Walzer, was known to have said, 'With the unknowledgeable rider the art starts at the horse's neck, and it also desists there . . .!'.)[1]

039
FORWARD AND DOWN

This exercise epitomizes one of the most important fundamentals of riding: that the horse learns to stretch its whole body forward in order to seek and find the bit correctly. It is a vital stage in putting the horse correctly 'on the aids'. It underscores the horse's self-reliance regarding its balance, whereby it learns to carry itself without seeking an artificial support in the reins. Furthermore, through this exercise the rider gains the necessary control over the full range of lengthening and shortening of the horse's frame; not to be confused with extension and collection of the gaits.

The forward and down exercise is not necessarily used only as a

[1] Meister der Reitkunst, Waldimar Seunig, Erich Hoffmann Verlag 1960.

transitionary stage in the training of young horses. One should be able to demonstrate 'forward and down' with any horse, at any stage of training. It will always remain for the rider tangible proof that his horse has been correctly worked, from back to front, and that its back muscles are elastically in play, originating from lively, impulsive hindquarters.

There are two main foundation stones on which the exercise is built:

1) Even rhythm, and the resulting relaxation, or unconstraint (030, logical sequence of training), so that the horse becomes 'driveable' (023).
2) The cardinal principle of bending: that in answer to the driving aids, the horse stretches the *outside* of its body when the outside rein is yielded forward, while the inside rein sustains passively, WAITING for the horse to soften to the bend.

Initially, young horses should be allowed and encouraged to stretch 'forward and down' at any time they wish. Once they become quite steady in the exercise, however, they should only be allowed down at the rider's request. As the rider gradually begins to yield forward with the reins (directly towards the horse's mouth only), care must be taken to keep the contact, and an even rhythm, while encouraging the horse *with the driving aids* to continue to stretch for the bit all the way down to the ground. *The horse's nose must remain at, or in front of, the vertical at all times.* One can easily either, a) prevent the horse from going down or, b) bring the horse's head back up to the correct position (poll the highest point), by increasing the driving, while maintaining the rhythm (052, the half-halt principle).

For both horse and rider, the exercise is best learned at the trot (rising trot for young horses). Once familiarity has been gained, the forward and down exercise can be practiced at the walk and canter as well. With older horses, best results can be achieved by doing the exercise with a full seat in all three gaits.

The exercise is best executed by using large, simple school figures, those which will not interfere with the smoothness of the work. At first it is best to use a 20 metre circle, changing the rein *out of the circle* every fourth or fifth round. If the horse is prone to rushing, put it on a smaller circle until a steady rhythm and a relaxed back have been well established. The circle should be enlarged when the horse becomes 'driveable' once again. Keep the following points in mind:

- Keep an even correct rhythm (relaxed horse!)
- Carefully drive the horse into lengthening its body, and stretching its neck to the ground. *The forward urge is the main ingredient to correct success.*
- The horse must have yielded to the bend by stretching the outside of its body and neck. It should not lean against the rider's inside leg.
- With a light, gentle hand bait the horse into stretching (this does not mean to fiddle with the bit) do not lose the contact.

Forward and down is not meant to be an exercise that releases the horse from the rider's controls, allowing it to merely dawdle along unbalanced on the forehand, nor should it stretch either because of laxity, or because of an evasive jerking-away of the reins (barging downward).

Once the rider becomes proficient at this exercise, it will be found to be enormously helpful to practise alternating frequently between riding 'forward and down' and putting the horse up 'on the aids'. Not only will this develop correct feels in the rider, but the gaits will also blossom beautifully.

040
EQUAL LOADING OF THE HORSE'S LEGS

Besides the equal loading of front and hind legs, which balances the horse and causes it to find the correct head position in self-carriage, the legs must also be laterally equally loaded: lateral equilibrium. If the horse is properly suppled and on the aids, this equal loading occurs automatically and naturally (044).

Indications of the horse *not* having equal weight on the inside and outside legs, are as follows:

- horse leaning on one rein

54

- horse's body bulging against one of the rider's legs
- horse going crooked
- head tipping, ears not on same level
- unlevel gait.

REFLECTIONS IV

– When training the horse: do little, and repeat frequently.

– Any artificial placement of the horse's head must be strictly avoided.

– It is damaging to the horse's gaits to ride *any* exercise in two-track work, turns on the haunches, or gaits other than *ordinary* walk, trot, and canter, unless the horse is first correctly put 'on the aids'.

– It must be repeatedly impressed on each rider, to instil his horse with the urge to move forward fluidly.

– *Let-throughable*: (permeable) that state in which the horse allows the energy from the hindquarters to flow through its whole body (035). This is an integral part of true suppleness.

– One will always be able to trace any riding problem to the breaking of one, or all of the cardinal rules of horsemanship: Forward, Calm, and Straight (029).

– If the horse is trained by force, force will be required to ride it.

– If the horse should become over-bent (the poll lower than the crest of the neck, and the nose behind the vertical), the driving aids must be used to raise the head to the correct position. Do not use the hand with sharp upward jerks.

– It is essential that the moment the horse yields to the rein pressure, the rider also instantly yields and becomes lighter with the hand (016, d). The same principle applies to leg aids.

– The most difficult task the horseman has to perform is to ride, purely and accurately, the three basic gaits 'on the aids'. Once this has been truly mastered, the advanced exercises are relatively easy, being a logical progression of *correct* basic work.

– When putting the horse 'on the aids' it is imperative to have it well *on* the inside leg and outside rein. This does not mean to take a

56

heavier contact on the outside rein, nor that we can abandon the presence of the other riding tools.

– When in trouble: do less! Neutralize. Let the horse settle down and find itself before making new demands.

– Use to your advantage *an isolation strip of time*, between old poor work and new better work; that is, stay at the same level of simple work (a few days, or weeks, or even months) until unwanted habits have been overcome. This applies particularly to badly spoiled horses.

– Attaining seat and leg obedience is the only genuine solution to gaining the horse's subsequent obedience and lightness to the reins.

Atlantis. Turn on the haunches, right.

CHAPTER V

THE EXERCISES; THE THREE GAITS; TWO-TRACK WORK; THE SCHOOL FIGURES

041
CATEGORIES OF EXERCISES

1) Loosening exercises:
(preparatory work)

- Walk on the loose rein.
- Rising trot.
- Turns on the forehand (sparingly).
- Leg-yielding (sparingly).
- Bending the horse left and right at the standstill, or while on straight lines at the walk and trot (NOT with young horses!) Read below.
- With some horses an easy canter for a few minutes (light seat).
- Frequent trot–canter–trot transitions.
- Forward and down riding (039).
- Use large, open school figures.

2) Suppling exercises:
(actual work starts here)

- Smaller school figures can be used, 10 metre circles, voltes, tighter serpentines, deeper into corners, etc.
- Frequent changes of rein.
- Riding positions right and left alternately on straight lines at walk and trot.
- Lengthening and shortening the stride in all three gaits.
- Frequent ridings of transitions.
- Halt and rein-back.
- Shoulder-fore at trot and canter.
- Shoulder-in, and counter shoulder-in.
- Counter-canter.

3) Collecting exercises: – Shoulder-in.
                           – Travers and renvers.
                           – Turns on the haunches.
                           – Halt and rein-back.
                           – Counter-canter.
                           – All suppling exercises can be included.

4) Collected work: – Three collected gaits.
(The High School   – Canter pirouettes.
of dressage.)   – Flying changes.
                          – Piaffe and passage.

5) The airs above the ground.

042

INTRODUCTION: THE PRACTICAL USE OF EXERCISES

Each day the horse is worked, it should be taken systematically and progressively first through the loosening, then the suppling, and finally (provided it is sufficiently advanced) the collecting exercises. It must demonstrate relaxation and willingness in each of these phases. If it does not, it should not be taken any further into more advanced or complex exercises until this basic correctness is achieved. Furthermore, it is a good practice to take the horse through a condensed version of its training programme to date, until those exercises are attained which are yet to be improved upon, or which have yet to be introduced.

Should one find a major discrepancy between the quality of one's basic schooling and one's attempts at advanced work, then either the basis is inadequate or incorrect, or the advanced work subscribes to false methods in an attempt to squeeze the much sought-after High School movements from an ill-prepared horse (rider). Unless the horse can demonstrate relaxed, pleasant 'simple stuff' in each riding session, *regardless of the level of its training*, it certainly will not be ready to do correct advanced work.

When the rider is as yet not sufficiently experienced, it is important to work with a clear, disciplined plan in mind. Though a bit of 'free' experimentation is always a healthy part of learning. Too much liberty, however, before some sound understanding is gained, leads only to indifferent results. Only the experienced rider can afford to (seemingly) flit about and do whatever is either necessary or possible at any given moment. This is so because of the rider's ability to sense continued correctness of freedom and balance in the horse outside the apparent success or completion of any particular movement. It would be very unwise for the beginner to ride in such a manner.

The riding sessions should be divided into suitable periods of work and rest. For unfit or young horses, a rough approximation could be anywhere from five to ten minutes of work followed by five minutes of rest (walk, on the buckle), with a total riding time of about half an hour. For older and more fit horses working periods can be expanded to fifteen or twenty minutes before resting for about five minutes, with a total riding time of about one hour.

The intermittent rest is important for both the physical and mental well-being of the horse, and also helps keep the rider's outlook fresh. With few exceptions, long, drawn-out sessions without rest tend to result in tired, inelastic muscles, and mental resistance in the horses.

It is a good practice to give the horses one regular day off work per week with turn-out in the paddock (more days off for young horses). Also, whenever possible, frequent hacking in the countryside is most beneficial to horse and rider.

043

ELABORATION ON THE LOOSENiNG EXERCISES (041, 1)

The main objective of the loosening phase is to let the horse find itself: allowing it to settle in, ridding its body of stiffness or discomfort from being in the stall, and becoming at ease with the rider's weight on its back. During these exercises, simple, large school figures should be used. Try to avoid sharp turns, or riding deeply

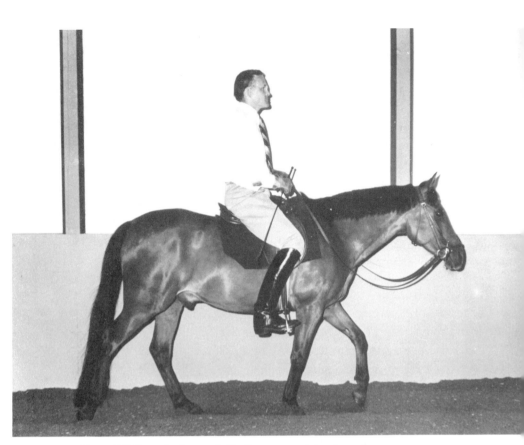

Barty. 'Walk on the loose rein' before any work has been done.

into the corners; and when changing the rein do so *out* of the circle or across the diagonals.

It is a sound practice to start each session with a few minutes of *walk on the loose rein* (on the buckle). It inspires confidence and relaxation in the horse, and serves the rider as a moment to settle down, and prepare mentally for the work to come.

Bending the horse slightly left and right at the standstill (be sure to use the appropriate seat and leg attitudes), serves to further the suppleness of the poll and jaw, and more importantly, it teaches both the horse and rider that the inside rein is used only to help bend the horse. It is not to be used to pull the creature about like a cart horse.

62

This exercise has little or no gymnastic value, and care must be taken to do it only slowly, deliberately, and sparingly at the halt. One can practise this more often and with less risk at the walk or trot, but take at least five or six strides to change the bend from one side to the other.

Leg-yielding and turns on the forehand must be practised sparingly; if not carefully used they can disengage the hindquarters. Leg-yielding has little gymnastic value. Nevertheless, the exercise can be used to advantage in the early training of the horse to teach it responsiveness to leg pressure (important!), or for limbering up during the warm-up. It is also very beneficial to the student, because it effectively teaches how to co-ordinate the symphony of aids: in particular it helps to clarify the concept of bringing the horse up to the outside aids, and how to receive it with the outside leg and rein. WHEN PROPERLY USED the exercise can also assist the rider in freeing the horse from hanging on the reins. When incorrectly or over-used, however, its effects can be devastating! Excessive use robs the horse of its forward urge, and can result in poor quality, broken gaits. Use with caution. The moment the horse responds willingly and lightly (usually after five or six steps), the exercise should be terminated.

Important points for leg-yielding and turns on the forehand:
- Only a very slight bend towards the leg you wish to yield away from.
- Increase the pressure in the yielding leg, and *think* of its diagonal partner the outside rein which must not be used actively, but be sure to 'have' it.
- Leg-yield at no more than a 45 degree angle to the track.
- *Absolutely equal pressure on both reins*: DO NOT PULL ON THE INSIDE REIN!! The horse must yield because of the leg pressure only.
- During turns on the forehand, stop and wait after each step, do not let the horse rush around. Once the rider learns how to receive the horse with the outside leg and rein, turns on the forehand in continuous motion may be practised.
- Sit squarely: *do not collapse in the hips*.

WHAT IS THE DIFFERENCE BETWEEN LEG-YIELDING AND SHOULDER-IN?

1) In leg-yielding the rider pushes the horse's hindquarters off the path taken by the forehand. It is initiated as a turn on the forehand while the horse is in forward motion, by pivoting the horse around the shoulder. Both front and hind legs cross over. There is only a slight bend through the horse. Its uses and value have been described above. The rider's yielding leg may be brought back by 4–5 inches while training the horse to leg-yield. Once the horse understands what is wanted, the rider's yielding leg should be close behind the girth.

2) In shoulder-in the rider RIDES the forehand slightly off the path taken by the hindquarters (starting the exercise by riding the first part of a volte, for example). This follows the most important fundamental principal of always riding the horse around the hindquarters, using them as a pivot. This is central to correct gymnastic training, being wholly harmonious with such engaging exercises as, turns on the haunches and travers. Only the front legs cross each other. The inside hind leg travels under the horse and towards the outside shoulder, and passes closely by the outside hind leg. The hindquarters remain on the path being ridden. There must be a very clear bend through the horse's body. The rider's inside leg should be close behind the girth, and his outside leg about a hand's breadth behind the girth. Important, see 055, which includes explanations of 3- and 4-track shoulder-in.

044

ELABORATION ON THE SUPPLING EXERCISES (041, 2)

The suppling exercises are used to establish the horse more solidly on the aids; initiating the elasticity in the horse's back; gaining control over the hindquarters, and therefore the balance; furthering the unity between horse and rider.

Supplling is best achieved through the full use of all school figures, with emphasis on bending the horse, and making frequent changes of rein. Work on circles is the first stage in moving the horse's centre of balance further back by increasing the load on one hind leg at a time (the inside one). The riding of transitions is particularly beneficial to suppling the horse.[i] Lengthening and shortening of the strides helps to ignite the forward urge and the balance which, in turn, prepares the horse for collection. The shoulder-in exercise is a helpful aid to achieving softness on the horse's stiff side (055).

The halt and rein-back help to sharpen obedience, they engage both hind legs simultaneously, as do turns on the haunches which further improve responsiveness to weight and leg aids. These turns are best when done from the trot: trot–halt–turn-on-haunches–trot-on again, all in one smooth motion. Do not linger at the halt for more than a moment.

- When executing turns on the haunches, heed the following points:
  (a) Keep the true forward intention (light, allowing hands). It is a serious mistake for the horse to step backward, or for the hind legs to stick to the ground.
  (b) Do not pull the horse around with the inside rein. The inside leg and seat bone (increased weight), and the outside leg and rein are the most important by far.
  (c) Keep each hand on its own side of the neck.
  (d) Sit squarely, do not collapse in the hips.
  (e) The correct sequence of walk steps must be maintained (044).

The practical value of all exercises is only realized if each rider, through methodical experimentation, discovers to which combination of loosening and suppling exercises his own horse responds most favourably. The immediate goal being, that the horse puts its body entirely at the rider's disposal in as short a time as possible – the blank cheque state.

The practical aims in suppling the horse are:

That the horse: (a) Moves freely and impulsively forward.

65

(b) Carries the rider equally well under both seat bones.

(c) Does not lean on one rein. Willingly bends to either side.

(d) Readily yields to leg pressure; does not lean on, or bulge against, one of the rider's legs.

The feeling of working a horse correctly is described in section 059.

045

AN INTRODUCTION TO THE THREE BASIC GAITS

Correct work produces gaits which take on an appearance of elastic ease. There is a clear roundness, a ground-covering springyness and fluidity in all movements. Harmonious effortlessness, borne out of balance and energetic vigour, are the chief hallmarks. If the gaits are to be considered correct by classical standards, they must demonstrate absolute purity of foot-fall, and be constant in rhythm regardless of the degree of extension or collection.

WORK AT THE WALK

Definition:	(a)	The walk has *steps*.
	(b)	It is a four-beat motion.
	(c)	No moment of suspension.
Sequence:		1. Right hind 2. Right front
		3. Left hind 4. Left front.

The sequence of steps at the walk must comprise a distinct and *deliberate* four beats, with an even, unhesitating rhythm. The walk is the least impulsive gait, it is the most difficult in which to keep a strong forward urge.

This gait can, however, be advantageously used by the student, in learning how to administer his aids without being unnecessarily tossed about. It is also beneficial to practise any new exercises at the walk with young horses, before the work is requested in the higher gaits.

66

It must be strictly observed to ride young horses at the walk on the long (or loose) rein only, until the second year of training. The youngster must first be well balanced and on the aids at the trot, before it should but put on the aids at the walk. The quality of the gaits can be permanently ruined if the horse is prematurely put on the aids at the walk. (Pace-walking can be one of the undesirable consequences.)

Modes of the walk:

Extended:	Hind foot steps well beyond front print.	
Ordinary:	Hind foot steps into or just beyond front print.	
Collected:	Hind foot steps short of front print; the motion is higher, rounder and more active.	

046

VALUE OF 'WALK ON THE LOOSE REIN' WITHIN A WORKING SESSION

Besides the obvious value as a moment of rest for both horse and rider, the walk on the loose rein (on the buckle!) serves to *renaturalize* the horse, which may have become uncomfortable or resistant. It is also a helpful solution to those moments when one's blood boils due to frustration; the walk on the loose rein can give the rider a clean slate after a period of cooling-off. After walking on the loose rein for a few minutes, one should take note of the smoother motion and the longer, easier stepping. When taking up the contact once again, care should be taken to preserve this fluidity.

While letting the reins out through the fingers, always *drive* the horse into lengthening its neck forward and downward. The horse should gradually lengthen itself, as opposed to jerking the reins from the rider's hands. Should the horse jerk hard, do not fight it directly with a hard, resistant hand; instead, keep the wrist, elbow, and shoulder relaxed, and give the horse nothing to fight against, and just drive a bit more. One could also place the hands on the withers or on the saddle; horses soon stop jerking when they realize they are

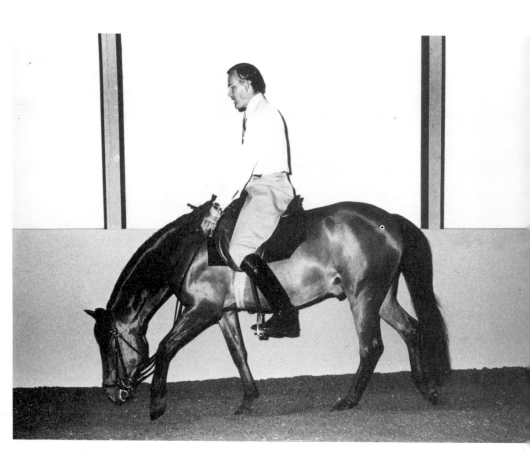

Barty. After some loosening exercises the horse drapes itself from relaxation. The horse stretches itself readily as the rider yields with the hands while driving. This attitude should be assumed any time. 'Walk on the loose rein' is ridden within a working session.

pulling on themselves. (The cause for jerking can lie in a lack of suppleness and forwardness in the horse; or from imbalances between the driving and receiving aids; or from poor hand attitudes.)

When riding on the loose rein, the horse must be kept moving freely forward, think of the *flow*.

047
WORK AT THE TROT

Definition: (a)   The trot has *strides*.
                     (b)   It is a two-beat motion.

<table>
<tr><td></td><td>(c)</td><td>A moment of suspension after each stride.</td></tr>
<tr><td></td><td>(d)</td><td>The presence of diagonal unison is of utmost importance. This means that within the motion of any diagonal pair of legs, both legs must leave the ground (or alight on the ground) at exactly the same moment. If the diagonal legs are not unified, an incorrect 3- or 4-beat motion results. See plate on page (110).</td></tr>
<tr><td>Sequence:</td><td colspan="2">Diagonal pairs of legs move alternately. There is a moment of suspension (no feet touching the ground for an instant) after each stride.</td></tr>
</table>

The bulk of riding should be carried out at the trot. It is the schooling gait for both horse and rider. The work at both the walk and canter will usually only progress favourably once the trot work becomes mature. The trot is more impulsive than the walk. It is the best gait for teaching the horse to balance itself, first on the longe, later under the rider; learning to respond to the activating aids, becoming supple and using its back and hindquarters.

The rider's seat and position will only develop correctly after much work at the sitting trot without stirrups, or being longed (but see 066, regarding use of young horses). Generally, once the rider has developed a good seat at the trot, then sitting well to the walk or canter poses few problems.

<table>
<tr><td>Modes of the trot:</td><td>Extended:</td><td>Hind foot can step as much as 36 inches or more beyond the front print.</td></tr>
<tr><td></td><td>Middle:</td><td>An energetic long trot, showing much knee and hock action. The hind foot steps well beyond the front print.</td></tr>
<tr><td></td><td>Ordinary:</td><td>(Working trot.) Hind foot steps</td></tr>
</table>

into or just beyond the front print.

Collected: Hind foot steps short of the front print. Croup lowered, a higher, rounder very energetic motion. The rhythm remains even, however, and the motion is neither hectic nor tense.

048
WORK AT THE CANTER

Definition:
(a) The canter has *jumps*.
(b) It is a three-beat motion.
(c) A moment of suspension after the third beat.
(d) The horse is on the correct lead when the inside front leg is leading (unless counter-canter is asked for).

Sequence:
1) Outside hind foot.
2) A diagonal pair of legs (inside hind foot, outside front foot).
3) Inside front foot; then the moment of suspension.

By its very nature, a series of jumps, the canter is the most impulsive gait. Nonetheless, special care must be focused on maintaining the true forward urge. It is a common mistake to slow the rhythm down, or worse yet, to attempt to collect the gait through the active use of the reins only (the backward-working hand). The horse invariably falls on the forehand, and due to a combination of inactivity and tensions, the gait breaks apart: the diagonal pair of legs (second phase) no longer move simultaneously, and an incorrect four-beat motion results.

COUNTER-CANTER: At the counter-canter the horse leads with

its outside front leg. (e.g. The right front leg leads while riding on the left hand in the school.) The horse should always be bent in the direction of the leading leg. Counter-canter is both a collecting exercise, excellent for suppling, and a preparatory exercise for flying changes of lead.

DISUNITED OR CROSS-CANTER: This occurs when the horse switches its lead behind (or in front) only. For example, the forehand leads right and the hindquarters lead left, or vice versa. This usually happens because the rider's seat is tense or unquiet, or his outside leg is not held clearly back (supporting the quarters), or because of imbalance or tensions in the horse.

Note: During any canter work the rider must keep the horse truly straight. Most horses tend to evade the honest loading of the inside hind leg by bringing the quarters toward the inside, it is a very common mistake. For sufficiently advanced riders, it is helpful to ride the horse in a *slight* shoulder-fore position as a correction for the 'croup-in syndrome'.

Modes of the Canter:	Extended:	Horse gains much ground at each stride, it must still be a three-beat motion.
	Middle:	A strong, impulsive canter, not fully extended.
	Ordinary:	(Working canter) The bulk of canter work should be executed at this gait. The length of stride should be a bit stronger than the horse might offer naturally.
	Collected:	The jumps are shorter and higher; not much ground is gained; the croup is well lowered and engaged. It must be a fluid, springy three-beat motion, not tense or choppy.

049

THE CANTER AID

The horse must be well prepared, and responsive especially to bending aids, i.e. it must be supple.

(a)   Horse clearly bent around the inside leg.

(b)   Inside leg in the normal position near the girth, outside leg well back (be aware of weight through the lowered heel) 027.

(c)   Inside seat bone slightly forward, and with a bit more weight in it.

(d)   Let the horse through the light hands as the seat and inside leg say, 'Canter on!' The outside leg gives the same pressure but is held passive. A half-halt is given just before the aid to canter-on; this balances the horse and frees it from the hand. Clearly lighten the inside rein at the canter strike-off.

(e)   To maintain the canter, the aid to 'canter on' is repeated at each stride (to a greater or lesser degree).

Be cautious not to force or surprise the horse with the canter aid, as tensions and rushing will result. With young horses it is best to strike-off to the canter from the trot, using the corner of the school to help juggle-up the correct lead. One may need to reinforce the canter aid with the stick (either at the horse's inside shoulder, or behind the rider's outside leg), until the horse becomes familiar with the signal from seat (weight aid) and leg. One should not strike-off to the canter from the walk until well into the second year of training; the horse should first be well established in walk 'on the aids'.

It is a common mistake to force the horse back into the canter immediately after it has fallen from the canter into an unbalanced, rushing trot. When this happens, the rider should instead always take the time to bring the horse into a good, rhythmic, relaxed trot before striking-off at the canter once again. With more advanced horses one should make the transition down to the walk before commencing with the canter again; this improves the balance, suppleness and use of the back, and the engagement of the hindquarters.

Should the horse strike-off on the wrong lead, don't get rough with it, snatching it back sharply to the trot or walk. Instead, use this mistake to your advantage. Only a fool rejects a happy accident! Ride the counter-canter for a few moments *deliberately*, it will help to supple the horse. Then patiently bring it through the downward transition, and try the correct lead again. Only adequate preparation (suppling) will produce the correct lead consistently.

050
TRANSITIONS

All transitions, both the lengthening and shortening of the stride within the gaits, going from gait to gait, and the making of half-halts at any time, are occasions when the rider must further activate the horse. Transitions must be decisive, fluid, and forward in nature. They should give the work an appearance of seamlessness.

By and large, a transition or the respective, resulting gait will be only as good as the work in the previous gait.

'Single' transitions are a simple progression, for example: halt to walk, walk to trot, and trot to canter. 'Double' or 'triple' transitions entail skipping interim gaits, for example: halt to trot, or walk to canter, or canter to halt, etc. Use only the 'single' transitions for young horses.

051
THE HALT

An experienced rider on a well-suppled horse can demonstrate halts, half-halts and rein-back with a feather-light contact. In a correct halt the horse should come to stand squarely and quietly on all four legs. An unsquare halt is a sign that the horse was not truly supple, and that it was not stepping up to both sides of the bit evenly before the halt was executed.

Atlantis. The halt. The horse is held 'at the aids' with seat and legs, the hand remains passive.

A truly correct halt can only be executed on a horse which is sufficiently active, supple, and well on the aids (balanced), with a swinging back, whereby the 'circuit' can become complete, (035). The rider must drive the horse (passively) up to a restraining hand. The hand must filter the forward energy in a soft, elastic way. *This is strictly an attitude of the hand, and does not constitute a pulling in any sense of the word.* The hand should also not become hard and fixed, thereby snubbing-off the impulsion, making it impossible for the hind legs to remain engaged.

When correctly executed, the halt (and rein-back) can be an effective key to the increased loading of the hindquarters, and also improves the general obedience of the horse. While halting or performing a half-halt, the rider must keep his head up and have a well stretched position (005, 009, 014).

052
THE HALF-HALT

The half-halt is foremost a balancing tool. It is the main key to harmony between horse and rider, and one of the most important avenues to liberating the horse's powers. Only via this freedom, founded on balance, can true suppleness and self-carriage be achieved. The half-halt gives the rider the possibility to reactivate the horse, gaining a more springy stepping, without changing the rhythm while in motion. It therefore helps the rider maintain the horse's centre of gravity beneath his seat, without the horse taking the hand (leaning). The half-halt serves both as an introductory signal and a preparation for the horse before corners, before changing the bend, and before all transitions.

For the half-halt to be correct and effective the horse must be responsive to the forward driving aids. Only once the horse has responded to the active driving aid from the legs (always supported by the seat) by filling the reins with forward energy, should the hand offer a momentary resistance (for no more than one stride), and then allow the horse forward again, as the *seat alone* continues to urge the horse on. Two points must be heeded: 1) after the half-halt, the hand should only assume an *attitude* of allowing: do not lose the contact, nor let the horse come off the aids; and 2) it is essential that the active driving aid from the legs stops immediately when the horse has responded to them. The calves should cling lightly, passively, and relaxed on the horse's sides at that time, preventing the newly-gained balance and energy from creeping out from underneath the seat bones.

If the half-halt succeeds, the horse will respond to the restraining effect by gathering itself up under the rider's centre of balance, 'filling' the seat, and by becoming lighter on the contact. Should it not succeed, then tune the horse once again to the driving aids, and try again; it may be repeated as frequently as necessary to achieve the desired animating/balancing results.

Be sure not to fall victim to the pitfall of half-halting with the hand alone (the backward-working hand), without initially having obtained an adequate response from the seat and legs. Also the half-halt should never degenerate into a crass jerking on the outside rein; at most it is a little squeeze *within the outside fist itself*. It is highly undesirable to move the bit around in the horse's mouth incessantly. It makes the mouth insensitive, whereby ever more and stronger aids need to be given to achieve any effects. Active rein aids should only be used deliberately, *when necessary*, not just for good measure. When the horse is adequately prepared (is obedient to the seat and legs, and is suppled and willing to bend, and correctly 'on the aids'), the half-halt can be executed without an active hand altogether, using the driving aid from seat (braced back) and leg, and then receiving that energy with a *momentary and passive* resisting attitude in the hand. The driving aid predominates and outlasts the rein influence, after which the rider neutralizes, and the seat flows freely with the horse's movement once more.

It is helpful for beginners to learn how to perform the half-halt by *thinking* of making a downward transition. For example, at the walk, the rider should think of coming to a halt, but just before the horse actually comes to the halt, the hand yields thus allowing uninterrupted forward motion ... as the seat reconfirms the forward motion. At the trot, the hand would yield just before the horse is about to walk; at the canter, one would yield with the hand just before the horse breaks into the trot.

This is, of course, a very exaggerated exercise, and it should only be used temporarily. The rider should learn to perform half-halts in a much more subtle way, so that the observer cannot see the horse so drastically changing its pace. Ideally, the horse must stay in the same rhythm, and the observer should only see a greater activity and elasticity of the hindquarters, and an overall improvement in the horse's balance. Practising 'single' transitions (trot–walk, walk–trot,

76

or walk–halt, halt–walk) can also initially be a helpful key to coming to understand how to execute correct half-halts. In this case, particular attention must be given to crisp, active upward, and smooth 'yielded' downward transitions. Also remember, either active hand, or active leg (with engaged seat); do not use both *actively* at the same time. One may, for example, drive passively and elastically with the engaged seat and clinging legs as the hand (outside rein) half-halts actively; or conversely, one may resist elastically and passively with the reins as the seat engages and the inner leg drives actively.

- The rider's driving aids say, 'a bit more activity'. (Clearly stretch the upper body, and look to the horizon.)
- The hand says, 'but stay in rhythm' (then yields).

The motto for the half-halt is:

- DRIVE ... RECEIVE (RESIST) ... BECOME LIGHTER AGAIN ...

(Important, regarding seat attitudes, see Chapter 9.)

053
THE REIN-BACK

The rein-back originates from the passive driving aids. In this case, however, the seat is lightened by bringing the upper body *slightly* forward from the waist (keep the seat bones on the saddle). This opens the back door, and allows the horse to go backward.

The rider's legs say, 'move ...'

All the hands say is, 'not forward'. The hand is strictly *not* to pull the horse backward, though small alternating *feels* may be given on the reins in time with the stepping of each corresponding hind foot.

To stop the rein-back, the rider closes the back door by sitting upright again, presses his seat bones into the front of the saddle and emphasizes the legs, while clearly yielding with the hands (do not lose the contact, nor throw away the 'carriage' of the horse).

The correct rein-back is constituted in an absolutely pure diagonal stepping: a two-beat motion, without a moment of suspension. If the horse has a resisting back, or if the rider's hand actively pulls back,

an incorrect four-beat motion results. The horse's legs must be picked up clearly. Dragging feet is a sign of incorrect work. i.e. resistance or tensions.

To use more than 5–6 steps of rein-back at any one time would constitute a punishment. Making any more than 10 steps backward becomes unacceptable, because it endangers the tendons and joints which can suffer damage from such senseless practice.

Both the halt and rein-back must be executed with a straight horse; any lateral evasions must be carefully prevented. (Diagonal aids.)

Upper. Barty. Rein-back. Here the horse is showing difficulties in its back, indicated by the relatively open position of the head/neck, and the stiffness in its front legs which appear to be stuck to the ground. Its non-yielding attitude is also mirrored in its unhappy facial expression.

Lower. Atlantis. Rein-back. Here a more advanced horse in exactly the same rein-back phase as the upper photo. Showing a good attitude psychologically, and a correct yielding attitude of the neck (back). The rider is just in the process of erecting the upper body and bracing the back to come to the halt. Comparatively, the upper photo shows clearly the 'unloading' of the horse's back (rider leaning forward) during the actual process of reining-back. In both photographs a correct diagonal stepping is illustrated.

054

THE DEFINITION OF TWO-TRACK WORK

Any work which is not ridden straight (i.e. on a single track, 029) is referred to as two-track work, this is irrespective of whether the horse's legs make three or four separate tracks. The issue is that the forehand and hindquarters each travel on their own separate paths.

Correct two-track work should not be confounded with an uncontrolled crookedness which the horse might offer as an evasion. It is not recommendable for the beginner to practise any two-track work, the sparing use of leg-yielding excepted, until he is very thoroughly acquainted with riding the horse 'on the aids', in all simple school figures and in the three basic gaits; riding these perfectly straight *on a single track* (029).

It is beyond the scope of this brief text to engage in a detailed study of the value of all two-track work. However, the most significant foundation, which is shoulder-in, will be fully described. Basically, two-track work should not be used as an end in itself. There is nothing particularly noteworthy about being able to make a horse go sideways. Though it is requested in many dressage tests to demonstrate the rider's control, it is critical to understand that ANY and ALL exercises we do should be aimed at one, and one goal only: The improvement of the quality and purity of the three basic gaits IN SINGLE-TRACK WORK!

Two-track work can be validly implemented by experienced riders to further the suppleness of the back, and hindquarters, and to improve on the general malleability and balance of the horse. Under the guidance of an instructor two-track work can also be a helpful learning tool for sufficiently advanced students.

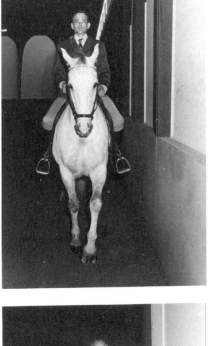

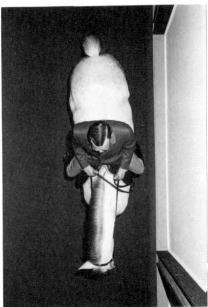

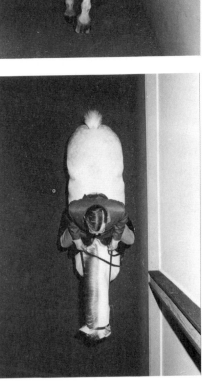

Work on the straight line (029, 056). From above, the rider's hips and shoulders are exactly square, sitting over the centre of the horse. When observing the horse from the front, one should see only TWO legs.

Position right. It should be noted that in all these photos, the horse travels parallel to the school walls.

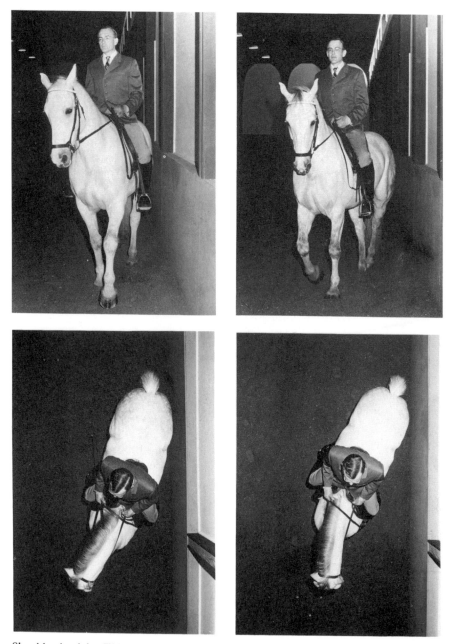

Shoulder-in-right. This represents the SECOND POSITION. (See foot note 055).

Renvers. (The reverse exercise to travers).

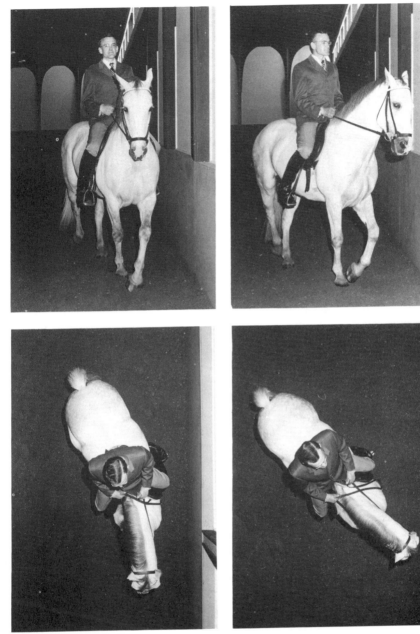

Travers right. (When practised across the
diagonal of the school it is called
HALF-PASS).

Leg-yielding, away from the left leg. (Can
also be practised with the horse facing
toward the inside of the school 043).

055

SHOULDER-IN
OF WHAT VALUE IS THE SHOULDER-IN EXERCISE?

(a) It helps the rider supple the stiff side of his horse, and therefore contributes to the straightness. (In this instance the exercise might be considered a very mild form of leg-yielding.)

(b) It helps to put the horse more clearly onto the inside leg and outside rein.

(c) It helps to further the horse's balance, and the suppleness and activity of the hindquarters. It can therefore be used as a collecting exercise. *Take note, however, that these effects can only be gained from a horse that has first been well prepared and put correctly on the aids in single-track work.*

(d) It is the basic preparatory exercise for all other two-track (lateral) work in all three gaits. Every step of half-pass and turns on the haunches, for example, should have the 'seed' of shoulder-in wholly entrenched within it.

TECHNICAL REQUIREMENTS (a description of the full shoulder-in, or *second position*).[1]

(a) The exercise is ridden on three tracks. The outside hind foot makes one track; the inside hind foot follows exactly in the path

[1] THE FIRST POSITION, or shoulder-fore, is a preparatory exercise for shoulder-in, it is basically the same exercise as the second position but the horse does not come off the wall quite so far. In the first position the inside hind leg travels in a path that runs exactly between both front legs. Its aim is to achieve a sound bend, and to cause the hind legs to travel closer together, which is the basis for improving balance and control.

of the outside front foot, making the second track; last, the inside front foot makes the third track.

(b) The horse must be bent through its whole body. As much bend as possible in the body, take care, however, not too much bend in the neck.

(c) The hindquarters travel straight along the wall. Only the forehand is brought slightly over to the inside of the school.

THREE-TRACK VERSUS FOUR-TRACK SHOULDER-IN

Some classical masters have recommended shoulder-in to be done on four tracks, with the forehand yet further from the wall than is described above (both front and hind legs crossing). In this case, it is not a question of 'right' or 'wrong', it is a matter of classification. This author shares the view that any angle beyond three tracks would become a form of leg-yielding (but with more bend through the body). The four-track work is therefore not necessarily 'incorrect', after all, leg-yielding is not considered 'incorrect'. So of course one can use it, but it does not bring the same suppling and collecting effects as the three-track shoulder-in. Each has its own perfectly valid effects; yet neither one can fully replace the other. It is a matter of finding out which one will bring desired results from the horse at any given moment. The following points give guidance:

(a) A horse which is not yet 'fully there' might benefit more from the occasional bit of leg-yielding with more bend through the body (call it four-track shoulder-in if you will!).

(b) As is commonly accepted, the horse will not benefit from three-track shoulder-in unless it has already found suppleness and balance.

(c) The clincher is, however, that once the horse IS well supplied and balanced, then, without a doubt, the three-track shoulder-in will continue to develop the horse, where the stronger-angled work would become an impediment to achieving the higher degrees of true collection.

Regardless of which of these exercises we use, great care is advised in its use. The most important issue is HOW we use this work, and that it truly improves on the horse's way of going.

PRACTICAL IMPLEMENTATION (Applies to all two-track work)

(a)   For any two-track work it is essential that the horse goes more forward than sideways.

(b)   The horse must be 'on the aids' before attempting the exercise (active and balanced).

(c)   Care must be taken to remain sitting squarely in the saddle. Do not collapse onto the inside hip.

(d)   Start the exercise after the second corner of the short side of the school, or from a volte. Do not wrestle the horse into a shoulder-in position with the reins, rather, *ride* the forehand off the wall, as though you want to go into the school. As the forehand starts to come off the wall, indicate to the horse that it should go along the wall at the desired angle by giving a half-halt, then emphasize the inside leg and *feel* the outside rein (equal weight in both reins anyway!). The inside leg, which should act behind the girth, tends to both the forward and sideways motion. The rider's outside leg, placed about a hand's-breadth behind the girth (and in conjunction with the outside rein), fulfils the critical function as *passive receiving agent* of the horse, while also *passively* driving the horse forward. Always be sure to have the horse well sandwiched between both reins and legs, and never to ride with just one rein or leg. This is particularly important for turns on the forehand, turns on the haunches, or any two-track work.

(e)   If a problem arises (crookedness, resistance or constrained forward motion, unlevel gaits) the horse must be corrected by suppling in *single-track work*. Go immediately onto a large circle, and ride the horse forward until the gaits become pure and active once again.

(f)   Shoulder-in, as with all two-track work, must be practised with great discretion. The bulk of our work should be carried out on a single track. The horse's gaits, especially the forward urge, suffer adversely when two-track work is practised incorrectly or superfluously.

056
THE IMPORTANCE OF RIDING ON 'STRAIGHT LINES': SINGLE-TRACK WORK

Bending exercises are used to supple, in order to be able to straighten the horse (029)! It is essential that plenty of work on ruler-straight lines also be ridden; on the second track, across diagonals, and the centre line (away from school walls), this is particularly important for young horses.

While riding on straight lines, the rider must sit exactly square in the saddle, with both legs in the same position (the outside leg is not brought back, unless *momentary* correcting aids need to be given; or when riding in 'position' [see photographs on page 81] while on straight lines).

057
OF WHAT VALUE IS THE RIDING OF SCHOOL FIGURES?

The accurate riding of school figures gives the rider the essential *purpose* whereby he can assess his riding and evaluate where his control is lacking. Flitting about aimlessly has little or no schooling value for either horse or rider. Furthermore, when the figures are ridden 'Forward, Calm, and Straight' (029), they become a valuable tool in helping the student to put his horse on the aids correctly.

058
THE SCHOOL FIGURES

The school figures should be practised equally on both hands in order to exercise and develop the complete muscle structuree, balance, and ambidexterity of the horse.

There are certain factors concerning the riding of school figures which require some explanation.

(a) With the exception of the initial 'loosening' work, it is important to ride well into the corners of the school. Here the rider can learn to bend the horse around his inside leg, and ask for activity without the horse rushing away from the driving aids. Take note, however, that with unbalanced, young horses, the corners should be well rounded-off, especially at the trot and canter.

Remember to prepare the horse well BEFORE the corner by riding in 'position', give a half-halt, then LET the horse through the corner while emphasizing the driving aids.

Essentially, a corner is well ridden before the corner, not IN

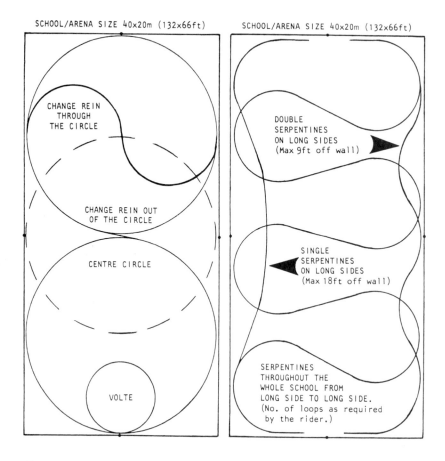

SCHOOL/ARENA SIZE 40x20m (132x66ft)   SCHOOL/ARENA SIZE 40x20m (132x66ft)

CHANGE REIN THROUGH THE CIRCLE

CHANGE REIN OUT OF THE CIRCLE

CENTRE CIRCLE

VOLTE

DOUBLE SERPENTINES ON LONG SIDES (Max 9ft off wall)

SINGLE SERPENTINES ON LONG SIDES (Max 18ft off wall)

SERPENTINES THROUGHOUT THE WHOLE SCHOOL FROM LONG SIDE TO LONG SIDE. (No. of loops as required by the rider.)

the corner itself, when it is too late and only brings tensions in the horse.

(b) While riding on large circles, an excellent exercise to practise is to make the circle smaller by gradually spiralling towards the centre (moving the horse away from the outside aids) until the circle is *volte* size, then enlarging it once again to full size (by pressing the horse out, away from the inside leg).

(c) The riding on the second track (six to eight feet from the school walls, and parallel to the walls), is an ideal exercise to emphasize the need to contain the horse within the rider's 'river banks' at all times (032). While practising this exercise the rider should ride diligently into the *imaginary* corners.

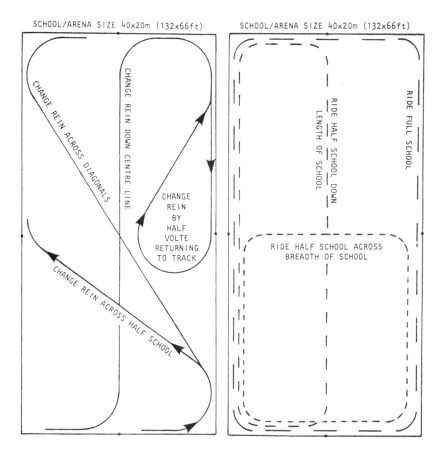

SCHOOL/ARENA SIZE 40x20m (132x66ft)   SCHOOL/ARENA SIZE 40x20m (132x66ft)

CHANGE REIN ACROSS DIAGONALS

CHANGE REIN DOWN CENTRE LINE

CHANGE REIN BY HALF VOLTE RETURNING TO TRACK

CHANGE REIN ACROSS HALF SCHOOL

RIDE HALF SCHOOL DOWN LENGTH OF SCHOOL

RIDE FULL SCHOOL

RIDE HALF SCHOOL ACROSS BREADTH OF SCHOOL

REFLECTIONS V

– Correct transitions are the proof of the pudding.

– Always bend the horse in the direction you are going. The only exceptions are: 1. Shoulder-in 2. Leg-yielding 3. Counter-canter.

– When riding any curved lines the horse must be bent throughout its whole body, not just at the head and neck.

– In doing any two-track work remember to let the forehand ahead. The horse must move *forward-sideways*, rather than *sideways-forward*.

– Simplicity is the strength of the exercise.

– Always ride the forehand around the hindquarters. When straightening the horse, line the shoulders up with the hindquarters, rather than trying to push the quarters about to line up with the forehand.

– It is incorrect to press the horse towards the outside of a circle or turn, or ride into a corner, by pressing the inside rein against the neck. It is a sign that the inside leg is not doing its job, and that the horse is also not *on* the outside rein correctly.

– Only when we ourselves become truly ambidextrous, can we expect our horses to work equally well on both reins.

– Advanced work is only ever as good as the basics.

– The stability and balance in the horse can only be established through a resolute forward urge. This is fundamental in maintaining the purity of the gaits.

– Do not work the horse more on its difficult side; work it equally on both reins. Frequent changes of rein 'brings home the bacon' faster than dogged grinding on the weaker side.

– Ultimately, a smooth performance is made up of a continuous series of minor corrections, before major problems have manifest themselves.

– The rider should always determine the exact length of stride to be ridden, and not just go around in some ill-defined gait.

Barty. Working canter.

CHAPTER VI

GENERAL OBSERVATIONS

The prime task of dressage riding is to assist the horse to move more efficiently and beautifully while carrying the rider. However, to toy with the horse's basic nature is a complex serious undertaking that must be dealt with very carefully and respectfully. It is far easier to detract from the horse's natural beauty than to enhance it. Thus before the rider can hope to improve on the basic gaits he must acquire a reasonable understanding of the raw material with which he is working.

So long as the rider simply 'hacks' his horse around inoffensively, leaving the horse to its own devices, he will likely neither harm, nor improve the motion of the three basic gaits. He will also, however, not cause the undesirable effects which result from using methods which are in conflict with the creature's nature.

While learning how to influence the horse correctly, the rider can avoid going seriously off-track by becoming acquainted with the signals given by the horse, indicating its happiness or dissatisfaction with the language (aids) the rider is using, and the work and exercises being asked of it. The next two sections outline these aspects in detail.

059
WHAT ARE THE SIGNS OF CORRECT WORK?

- The first sign that the horse is beginning to relax, and use its muscle ring, is that it starts to snort or 'blow'.
- The horse's back wells-up beneath the rider's seat. The rib cage fills, making it easier to keep the legs on, and enables one to ride correctly with the shins (instead of the back of the leg or heels).
- The supple, swinging back becomes easy to sit on, and carries the

rider evenly under both seat bones. The tail swings gently with the motion.
- The gaits become rounder, more clearly cadenced, springy.
- The horse is in front of the rider's seat and leg; the forehand becomes large and light, because the shoulder is freed due to the supple, engaged and deep hindquarters.
- The horse becomes easy to keep straight. Halts are easily executed and square. Transitions are fluid and clean.
- There is a good, soft, elastic feeling in the hand.
- The horse responds well to the driving aids. Its whole body readily lengthens and the gaits lengthen when the rider's hands yield forward towards the bit. In both extension and collection the rhythm remains even, not erratic.
- The horse's facial expression is quiet and accepting.
- As a result of stretching for the bit, relaxation and activity, the horse begins to chew *quietly*, producing a *firm* foam on its lips. When the saliva is too watery it is usually a sign of nervousness, characterized by a noisy, exaggerated biting at the bit.

060–A
POINTS TO WATCH FOR IN INCORRECT WORK

PROBLEM	CAUSE[1]
- Stiffness, unwilling to bend.	- Tensions (060–B) in horse's back and neck, general resistance. Lack of suppleness, forward urge. Rough, dominant hands.
- Rough trot and canter; hard to sit on.	- Back not supple; circuit not complete; lack of activity; gaits broken apart.

[1] If the horse should not appear to be 'performing as usual', the rider should keep in mind the possibility that it might not be feeling 100 per cent well. It may be suffering from slight colic, cramps, stiffness, or might simply not be in 'good form' for whatever physical or psychological reasons. The horse is not a machine!

– Too fast a rhythm, rushing.	– Imbalance; tensions, discomfort, soreness, not relaxed in back; over-riding; insensitive driving.
– Grinding teeth, noisy biting at the bit; mouth open; unquiet expression in eyes.	– Horse unhappy; experiencing pain, or mental distress; lack of true forward movement; rider forcing; hard or dominant, or over-active hands.
– Swishing of tail.	– Mental resistance; rough aids; horse experiencing discomfort or pain, or is ticklish (caution with spurs).
– Horse boring on the hand (face often behind the vertical).	– Lack of activity, balance; horse rushing; on the forehand. Heavy or dead hands; rider stiff, or lacks independence of seat/upper body/hands.
– Crookedness	– Horse not framed and/or not supple. Horse pressed together too soon into collected work. Hand bottling horse up. Lameness.
– Tossing of head	– Lack of balance and/or discomfort in back; rider's hands too unquiet or hard. Bridle badly adjusted. Least likely, though possible, problems with teeth.
– Forging or 'clicking' (hind foot striking sole or shoe of front foot).	– Horse on the forehand, actively using hind legs, but its back is not in play (leg-goer). Least likely, shoeing or trimming job not suited to horse's build or way of going.

CAUSES OF RIDER-INDUCED TENSIONS IN THE HORSE

Though horses sometimes do use tension as a defence against the rider, in order to avoid going to work, and tension certainly can also be brought on by outside influences, the preponderant source of tension in the horse usually originates with the rider. The following are the most common causes:

- The rider's own fear or anxiety.
- The rider's own physical tension or stiffness.
- The rider's crookedness.
- The rider making a 'big deal' about anything.
- Any direct confrontation with the horse.
- Harsh, blunt, or insensitive use of any aids; especially the rein aids.
- Unfair or unreasonable use of whip or spurs.
- Inadvertent unbalancing of the horse, usually caused by the rider's own imbalance, or an inappropriate choice of school figures or exercises.
- Insufficient careful preparation each and every day, again, with a sound programme of loosening and suppling exercises.
- Pressing the horse too quickly in its general training programme, especially forced collection. *Over-facing!*

INDICATIONS OF TENSIONS IN THE HORSE

- The gaits lose their elasticity, becoming flat, jarring, expression-less, unsteady, erratic in rhythm.
- The horse's back becomes dead, difficult to sit on. The rider's legs can no longer hang effortlessly on the horse's sides.
- The feeling in the reins becomes dead, hard or empty.

061
ATTITUDES AND ANTIDOTES FOR NERVOUS, EXCITED, OR TENSE HORSES

- The rider must *melt*, that is, relax both mentally and physically.
- Have a soft, pliant seat. Rising trot may be advisable.
- Keep the legs on with a caressing attitude.
- Have a gentle, steady contact; possibly guide the hands on the neck; or take both reins in one hand and stroke the neck with the free hand.
- Keep the rhythm/tempo even: half-halt, don't hang on, keep the hands independent.
- Use simple school figures, and exercises, until the horse settles down. Use a smaller circle for a while.
- Pay no *direct* attention to the horse's excited state, concentrate instead only on your own relaxation and on the work at hand.

062
SHYING

- It is absolutely critical that the rider pays absolutely no attention to the real or imagined object the horse is shying from. Even if a bomb drops next to the riding school, as far as the horse should be concerned, *the rider can't see or hear anything!*
- Keep cool. Do not get emotionally involved. Be bored.
- Bend the horse *away from* the frightening object.
- Pass the 'bogie man' in a shoulder-in attitude.
- *As you approach and pass by the problem spot, relax the contact very deliberately (both hands).*
- Concentrate on the horse's obedience to the inside leg, but don't make a big issue about it, *especially not at the site of the shying.*
- Then tune the horse to the inside leg *somewhere else* in the school with a little bit of shoulder-in, and make a few more passes by the problem spot, making sure you very deliberately relax as you approach and pass by it, while keeping the legs on *gently and passively*, yet steadily.

– Praise the horse with either voice or stroking the neck *after* passing the problem area. Then forget about the whole issue completely! Act as though it never happened.

063

WHICH BITS SHOULD BE USED?

Most of the work in training of either horse or rider should be done with a plain, mild snaffle bit. Because the snaffle is broken in the middle, it can act unilaterally on either side of the horse's mouth: a pre-requisite in helping to teach the horse initially how to yield to the bending aids (a task which must originate with the seat and legs, which should always assume the pre-eminent role in bending). There is only one factor which determines the severity of the plain snaffle bit – the thinner the mouthpiece, the more severe the bit.

The double bridle is generally used as a formality in the showing of higher levels in dressage competitions. It is not necessarily a part of the horse's training; though it can, under certain circumstances, considerably alleviate the task in the *advanced* training of particularly resistant, bullish horses. Use of the double bridle during such training should be temporary: progress being frequently checked by testing the work on the snaffle. One should be able both to ride and train a horse through to the Grand Prix exercises on a plain snaffle bit.

The curb bit has a single unbroken mouthpiece. Its shanks are a lever which, via the curb chain as a fulcrum, put pressure on both the tongue and bars in the mouth. The curb bit can only be used as a restraining or receiving tool – regulating the pace or rhythm, and helping to maintain the balance in the horse. Therefore the bridoon is added, in order to facilitate control over the bend as well. To ride correctly on the curb alone, requires great experience, and the horse must be well prepared and supple as butter.

There are four factors that determine the severity of the curb – the thinner the mouthpiece (bar), the longer the shank, the larger the port, and lastly, the more tightly the curb chain is fitted – the more severe the curb bit.

With the exception of the above mentioned, no other bits have a place in riding or training in accordance with classical principles.

Having said this, it is important to add that the issue lies not so much in what we use as *how* we use it. An experienced rider can effectively use more severe bits, because he understands the full ramifications of the working of the whole horse. But the good rider can ride just as well with a mild bit. The advice to use mild bits for the students is certainly not aimed at denying them advancement. It is in fact a far surer guarantee of real progress, which does not originate at the bit in the first place!

It cannot be sufficiently strongly advised never to punish the horse with the bit. This practice must be considered a gross brutality! It is highly destructive to the gaits, and annihilates the horse's confidence in the rider. If punishment is absolutely necessary, a more effective and less damaging alternative is to discipline the horse with a smart whack with the stick (004, 21, punishment).

064
THE USE OF AUXILIARY TACK

- Draw-reins
- Chambon
- Side-reins (other than for longeing)
- Martingales (standing or running)
- German running reins
- Very sharp spurs

All of this auxiliary equipment, which is used to place the horse's head artificially, *has no place in the natural training of the horse.*

On very rare occasions, and then only in the most competent of hands, can side-reins or draw-reins be used *briefly* on badly spoiled horses which continually free themselves from the rider's aids by severe tossing of the head; or they can be used to help stabilize horses with particularly wobbly (spaghetti) necks. However, use should be discontinued as soon as possible; these artificial aids are a temporary means to assist the rider in eradicating specific problems. Frankly, the truly experienced rider never needs to use such auxiliary reins, realizing that they are a 'quick-fix', which do not actually assist in establishing sound, long-term results, and usually only cover up the symptoms of deeper, more fundamental problems.

Very sharp spurs are unhorsemanlike. The point at which an aid loses its effectiveness and becomes unacceptable, is when it starts to cause pain or actually damages the horse. (Where brutality begins, the art desists. E. von Neindorff.) It is important to interject that punishment, *per se*, has nothing to do with giving aids, and should similarly never cause physical damage. Generally, the spurs should be used to reinforce the sideways-yielding aids. The riding crop is a far more effective support for the driving aid because it directly initiates the horse's natural desire to flee. The spurs, on the other hand, by and large, cause the horse to withhold its fluid forward motion; they should be used sparingly and discretely.

065
LONGEING THE HORSE

All the principles of riding apply to longeing as well (029, 030). One needs a well-cultivated eye and an intuitive sense for the horse's motion to be able to influence it favourably and reap the benefit from the longeing work. Longeing and work-in-hand in general require special skills and talents. Not everyone who can ride well is able to longe well; conversely, some people who have a real knack for working the horses from the ground, can prove to be nothing more than mediocre riders. Certainly, having the horse merely twirling around, usually in too fast a rhythm, is a waste of time, and can be damaging to the horse's legs.

With regard to the adjustment of side-reins, there are too many variables in daily circumstances, and from horse to horse, to make any definite or pat recommendations. A fairly safe rule-of-thumb, however, is to end up having the horse's head in the correct position (034) when trotting. It is better to have the side-reins a bit too long than too short. It is very important that the handler knows how to match-up the level of impulsion with the level of compression set by the side-reins.

For some young horses, during approximately the first three to six weeks of longeing, the head should be adjusted to face slightly to the outside. As the horse learns to balance itself, one can gradually make both side-reins equal, and finally change the bend to the inside, on the circle line.

If at any time a horse (regardless of training level) should show resistance against the inside side-rein, *this should not be corrected by shortening the inside rein yet more*. The correct solution here is a patient and lengthy one. Both side-reins should be set longer *and absolutely equally*. The horse should be sent well forward, and coaxed into relaxing, and lengthening the outside of its neck and body. Only once the horse accepts both side-reins equally should the inside rein be slightly shortened once again.

The side-reins should be quite long for young horses, and their longeing sessions should always be started and ended with five to ten minutes *without side-reins*.

Make a habit of using either a longeing cavesson or a halter (over the bridle) for all longeing work. Do not attach the line to the bit, as it usually inhibits forward flow, and when in inexperienced hands, can cause the horse to become tense and distrustful of the bit. Also *do not jerk the horse around with heavy-handed snatches on the line*. It is ignorant, brutal, and a waste of time. If the horse is rushing, make the circle smaller for a while until it settles down, then gradually go larger again.

- *If the horse is lugging on the line*: this can be corrected best by STANDING IN ONE SPOT and repeatedly changing the *quality* of the contact on the line: HARD–soft, HARD–soft, HARD–soft. Do not pull back at all, and always end up with the soft, relaxed contact. Remember, horses can only lug when we give them something to lug on. Keep the horse moving fluidly forward.
- *If the horse is making erratic circles or cuts in*: STAND IN ONE SPOT. Start by making the circle a bit smaller. Keep the horse *in* on the side where it wants to cut out, while driving it carefully. On the other side where it wants to cut in, *do not drive*,

do not back up (stand your ground!), above all relax, and *ignore* the horse completely. It will take a few rounds to smooth the circle out. Only absolute steadiness and consistency of the handler's position and attitudes will bring success.

Be relaxed, calm and quiet in the middle of the longeing circle. Do not wander around. Keep the contact on the line elastic and light, with a relaxed wrist, elbow and shoulder, exactly as it should be during riding.

1) Longeing from the halter or cavesson, without side-reins or tack, is used for the following reasons:
   (a) The very first longeing sessions for the horse. The animal learns its first obedience, that is, going quietly around the handler on both hands without hindrance from tack, and establishing a regular rhythm at the trot. It learns the basic voice commands.
   (b) A method of free longeing for any horse, to give simple, controlled exercise.
   (c) Initial retraining for badly spoiled horses.
2) Longeing from the halter or cavesson with a bit and side-reins:
   (a) Establishes the balance, regularity and stability in the gaits.
   (b) The horse learns that the bit is to be *trusted* and respected. That the bit doesn't do anything as long as he yields through his entire body and searches for a contact on it. The horse quickly teaches itself not to pull against the bit provided that the handler does not interfere in any way, and merely assures that the horse continues to flow forward freely on a regular, smooth circle.

066
LONGEING THE RIDER

Much longeing without stirrups, especially at the trot, is a vital part of acquiring good physical habits, and excellence in our riding. It is an opportunity to put in extra effort to correct specific difficulties, which is often impossible under ordinary daily riding conditions.

 – The reasons for longeing the rider are:
   (a) Rider can concentrate solely on himself, while finding his balance, and harmony with the horse's movements.
   (b) Gain suppleness and independence of individual body parts.
   (c) Attain the correct position, which is an integral part of a good seat, and a suitable influence on the horse.
   (d) In keeping with the fact that the seat and position should be a wholly functional part in the giving of aids, the students should be made to keep the horse moving forward by themselves as much as possible (007).

– Which horse should be used to longe the rider?

> While longeing beginners, until they become acquainted with the horse's motion and gain confidence in coping with the unfamiliar task, a reliable, quiet, older horse should be used. As the student becomes more proficient, more volatile and energetic horses can be used.

– Important:

> In the first years of training, young horses should be spared this pounding-around on the longe, with riders doing sitting trot without stirrups. It is usually detrimental to the training, and can be damaging to the horse.

– Points of caution while longeing:

> – Have the longe line carefully organized (no knots or twirls). If the horse bolts, and the longe line is badly organized, the line can easily knot firmly onto the hand causing serious damage. *Always wear gloves while longeing!*
> – Always have the bridle reins tied up in such a way that the person being longed can use the reins to control the horse if something unforeseen should happen (line breaking, or coming loose).

REFLECTIONS VI

- An experienced rider doesn't need to use severe bits, an inexperienced rider certainly shouldn't use them.

- In the truest sense of the word the bit must remain the mediator between horse and rider, upon which neither may pull (neutral territory).

- The riding school should be a place of quiet work. Excessive noise in either the school or around the stables should be avoided.

- The horse should be tacked up carefully, with properly fitting tack. Carelessness can cause saddle or girth sores, or tossing of the head if bridles are uncomfortable or ill-fitted.

- Tighten the girth gradually, never over-tighten, as tensions will be caused in the horse's back; not to mention souring the creature.

- Be gentle while grooming, the horse is not a carpet! Remember, true horsemanship starts on the ground.

- It is not praise for the horse to get huge slaps on the neck or croup. Those who engage in this, usually only wish to advertise to the world how wonderful *they* are; it is senseless bravado. Stroking or patting the neck gently is far better received by the horse.

- Beginners aren't bad riders, they merely lack experience. The only truly bad riders are usually 'experienced' in the poorest sense of that word; those who blatantly and ignorantly bully their horses.

- Riding students, like horses, should be brought along within the limits of their own capability to learn. Requesting advanced work (to satisfy the ambitions of the instructor) without an adequate foundation, only forces the inexperienced rider into many poor habits, tensions, and contortions; not to mention the needless distress the horse is subjected to under such circumstances.

- Always be a friend to the horse's back (Egon von Neindorff).

Barty. Piaffe. Only through continued judicious exercising in the basics will improvement be realized in this advanced work. Though the quality of the contact is good, and the horse is pleasant in its neck and in expression (accepting), the stiff, unquiet tail indicates physical strain as the hindquarters commence to lower and bear more weight.

CHAPTER VII

THE SUBJECT OF PHOTOGRAPHY

067
THE ASSESSMENT OF HORSEMANSHIP IN PHOTOGRAPHY

For the experienced eye, a photograph of horse and rider is worth considerably more than a thousand words. Pictures reveal accurately the performance of both horse and rider at the particular moment the shot was taken.

One should certainly not condemn a rider on the strength of one photograph; everyone has a bad day or moment once in a while. The personal value in assessing equestrian photos lies in establishing more clearly in one's mind what the required standards of academic horsemanship are, thereby becoming more proficient in criticizing one's own work, and better equipped to improve on it. To sharpen one's perception for judging pictures, frequent practise is essential.

One should adhere to a set plan or evaluation to avoid the problem of trying to see everything at once, and end up seeing almost nothing at all.

068
SUGGESTED SEQUENCE TO FOLLOW IN ASSESSING PHOTOGRAPHS

1) General impression.
2) Technical points.
3) Purity of gaits.

069

GENERAL IMPRESSIONS:

FAVOURABLE ATTRIBUTES	POOR ATTRIBUTES
Pleasing	A forced appearance
Harmonious	Inharmonious, awkward
Balanced	Unbalanced
Elegant	Generally unpleasant
Beautiful	
The apparent ease of the performance	

070

TECHNICAL POINTS

(a) Correct position of the horse's head (034).

(b) Sufficient length in the neck.

(c) Flexion of the knee and hock of those legs suspended in the air (depends somewhat on the timing of the photo).[1]

(d) The horse must appear to be in front of the rider (up hill).

(e) Flowing tail carriage.

(f) Pleasant, quiet, accepting expression on the horse's face.

(g) Correct position and seat of the rider (see chapter 2).

(h) The pensive, composed, unforced appearance of the rider.

[1] One should always take into account the individual's build, suppleness and degree of training. A green horse, no matter how well ridden, will simply not look as good as a well trained horse in medium or advanced stages of dressage. Also, those horses with a round 'Hackney' motion, will generally make far more spectacular photos than those with a more flat 'daisy-cutter' motion. This difference is particularly evident in collected work.

The timing of the shot is pertinent to making a viable judgement. When taken too late, the front foot will already be on the ground. When taken too early, the legs will not be extended forward sufficiently to demonstrate the gait to best advantage. Therefore, the well-timed photo shows most clearly the desirable flexion of the knee and hock, and also the amount of leg activity.

071
PURITY OF THE GAITS

(a) Establish which gait is being portrayed.
(b) Check the purity of the gait:
  - walk, four-beat (045)
  - trot, two-beat (047)
  - canter, three-beat (048)
  - rein-back, two-beat (053)

(c) In extensions, the horse's whole frame must lengthen; the hind legs thrusting forward actively and purely.
(d) In collection, the horse must appear to be going uphill because of a supple back which results in lowered, more engaged hindquarters; flexion of the three major joints of the hind leg.

Note: In photographs there is little appreciable visual difference between medium and extended trot because the length of the moment of suspension does not show. At the medium trot the horse will already have almost fully extended its legs. That which differentiates the medium trot from the extended trot lies only in a more powerful thrusting-off of the hind legs, resulting in a more pronounced moment of suspension, and therefore a longer stride.

At the extended trot the front leg should point to the place where it will be landing; an exaggerated 'forward-upward' reaching of the forelimbs (goose-stepping) should be avoided. Ideally speaking, the front feet should not extend beyond the imaginary line drawn along the horse's face to the ground. However, some horses do display great freedom of the shoulder, and do extend the forelimbs somewhat beyond this line. This is acceptable provided that the requirement of diagonal unison is still fulfilled (047).

Any deviations from the exact, correct footfall must be deemed to be a deviation from the ideal standard of academic riding.

Meteorite. Incorrect work. An over-sp forehand at the extended trot. Note th the right front foot is still on the grou while its diagonal partner (left hind) is already airborne.

Meteorite. Incorrect work. An over-sp hindquarter at the extended trot. The right hind foot has landed long before diagonal partner, the left front. Such indications of tensions can be shown b any horse that is not supple. One's eye must be very sharply developed to be : to see these points while the horse is ir motion. Conveniently, the camera captures this split-second disharmony.

A fairly good demonstration of diagon unison at the extended trot. Note that gait is in general more elastic. This is shown in particular by the bend in the knee of the front leg. Compare this wi upper photos. The rider should not be leaning backwards.

072
INCORRECT WORK

Incorrect work invariably manifests itself in distortions of the gaits, usually because of either laziness or tensions. In both instances the horse doesn't step through its back.

LAZINESS: The horse may seem quite happy and the general appearance pleasant, however, one will be able to detect lagging hindquarters and imbalance in the horse, which drags itself around on the forehand, often boring on the rider's hands, sometimes with the face behind the vertical, and the poll not as the highest point.

TENSIONS: Almost without exception, tensions start in the horse's back, then manifest themselves in the poll and jaw and in the stiff tail carriage. As a result the horse no longer flexes the joints of its legs, and goes around 'peg-legged'; using its legs only, without the co-operation of a supple, elastic back. Such horses are referred to as 'leg-goers'.

073
THE SIGNS OF TENSIONS OR INCORRECT WORK

– Incorrect head position (034).
– Too short a neck in relation to the degree of extension or collection of the gait.
– The croup is high; the horse appears to be out behind the rider.
– Impure footfall in the gaits. The legs appear stiff.
– Crookedness.
– Tensions visible in the neck, poll, or jaw.
– Horse's neck broken or kinked at the third vertebra behind the poll.
– The tail carriage is stiff or swishing.
– The horse's mouth is dry. The lips are opened, snarling.

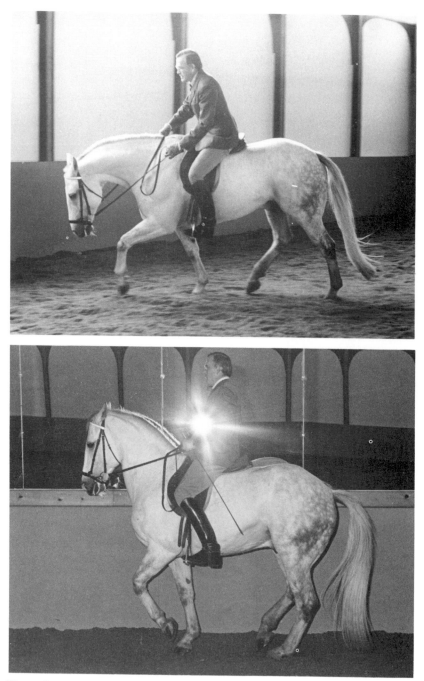

These photos portray Atlantis during Piaffe work. The corner-stone of correct work lies in the presence of the supple back. These photos illustrate this from, on the one hand (top), a soft stretching and yielding forward and down (the horse's nose should be pointing somewhat more forward) and on the other hand, the

supple deeply bent haunches in the Piaffe (bottom left). Compare the height of the tail from the ground. On the right hand page the horse is shown in a more advanced stage of the training, both in the snaffle and in a double bridle.

- The angry, unhappy or frightened expression on the horse's face and eyes.
- Poor position of the rider. (Chapter 2, 019, 020.)
- Any stiffness detected in the rider.
- Rider does not appear to be sitting *in* the horse; a general picture of disharmony and discomfort.
- Rider's facial expression strained.

THE OLD MASTERS

In the absence of living examples by which we can guide and rectify our riding (since most riders do not enjoy the opportunity to either see or work with teachers who are truly 'Masters'), we can still benefit greatly by making a regular habit of looking long and patiently at illustrations of the old masters. Many unspoken essences can be absorbed in this way. The rarity of such excellent examples should serve as a warning that we must remain ever vigilant about the quality of our work, if we ever wish to approach and uphold the ideals by which these masters measured their performance. Note especially the serenity which emanates from these photographs.

Richard L. Watjen, Middle trot. On 'Burgsdorff'. Beautiful harmony in motion.
Enormously impulsive, elastic, and forward.

Richard L. Watjen, Middle canter. On 'Feuerhorn'. Note the inclination of the upper body, in perfect dynamic balance with the moment.

Oberbereiter Meixner, canter pirouette left. On 'Favory Ancona'. The epitome of collection, bend, and deep flexion of the hindquarters.

Richard L. Watjen, Passage. On 'Burgsdorff'.

Oberbereiter Meixner, Passage. The finest example of the 'Long front line' of the upper body.

120

Part II

CHAPTER VIII

THE AIDS: PHILOSOPHY, ATTITUDES AND INFLUENCES.

This chapter contains both the practical and philosophical aspects encompassed in the giving of aids; our means of communication with the horse. It is aimed at developing suitable equestrian attitudes whereby the finer elements of conversation can begin to flourish.

In any communication it is equally as important to listen as it is to express oneself articulately. This certainly holds true for riding. In the presence of *the* expert on horsemanship – the horse itself – we should listen attentively, and allow all our senses to absorb as much information as possible before we venture to add to the dialogue ourselves.

Through careful analysis, while practising well-chosen exercises and accurate school figures, we can learn precisely what the interrelationships are between our aids and the responses they elicit from the horse. To gain fully from this work, however, we need to develop an intimate familiarity with the feeling for the balance of the horse within the three basic gaits. The walk, trot, and canter are the fundamental matrix of horsemanship. Only when we adhere to the purity and correctness of the gaits as our central guide can all minute alterations – good or bad, whether caused by the horse, the rider, or outside influences – be detected, and therefore be aptly reacted upon by the rider.

Though our messages are mainly transmitted via the horse's physical senses, we must avoid, at all costs, trying to move the horse's body and legs for it. Without a doubt the horse knows best how to implement its own powers. We can best awaken or direct these powers via *signals* that appeal to the horse's mind. These signals, or aids, are most effective when issued with minimal expenditure of our own physical energies. Furthermore, if the aids are to achieve desired results, they must be skilfully suited to the temperament, sensitivity, and level of development of each horse, and be appropriate to any given moment which can be blessed or plagued by circumstance.

Generally, aids are to be given in an explanatory manner, without force, and *without an edge on our aiding voice*. That is, we should be emotionally neutral. The aids are also more effective when given in a 'third person' mode. This means that our riding tools (and not we ourselves) are giving the commands to the horse. For example, we could be saying to the horse, 'This leg is asking you to yield away from it', instead of saying, '*I* am asking you to yield away from *my* leg'. This may seem an excessively fine point, but it will be found to be a very helpful attitude especially when we encounter difficulty. Not getting personally involved i.e., being void of egotism and emotion, is the crux of successful riding.

To give the aids from 'outside of ourselves', both physically and emotionally, liberates us so that we can truly remain a control centre, cool and detached, calmly in command of the situation. This is physically achieved by sitting as deeply, quietly and independently as possible, then (during aiding only) imagining the horse to be a hot potato, which we deftly juggle from aid to aid, to avoid getting burned by holding on too long, yet also not dropping it.

The principle on which aids function is based on the horse's natural tendency to yield to increases of pressure. Those horses which do not initially show this tendency can be very easily taught to yield by patiently practising the occasional turn on the forehand, and never by going directly against the horse's apparent intransigence. It simply does not yet understand that it can relieve itself from the rider's request by going where pressure is least. This precept is employed in practice by always leaving the horse an element of choice (the only exception to this is an irrevocable obedience to the forward driving aids, see section 023). Granted, the choice is made simple, but it remains a choice nonetheless. We achieve this by *passively* blocking-off all avenues except one: we make 'our way' the path of least resistance. Thus it becomes the horse's *will* to take that easier route, where it finds respite within our allowing neutrality and encouragement. Should a dictatorial, subjugatory attitude be used instead, however, then our work instantly assumes an adversary manner. Not only can this effectively teach the horse to seek self-protective evasions, but the horse is unlikely to willingly offer such a rider anything, and all work must be attained by force, or by the constant threat of pain.

The foundation from which all aids should be given is a *neutral basis* which has to find a place in both horse and rider. This state should be seen as a 'safe haven' from which we make brief, exact sorties of aid-giving, and to which we return immediately after the desired effects have been achieved: leaving the horse alone to do that which has been asked of it. This is the very nub of delegating responsibility to the horse, and optimizes the chances that it will offer, from its own initiative and wonderful child-like eagerness, that extra spark of brilliance to the performance.

The rider's neutral basis is a state of pure non-influence; a quietness, founded on harmony, devoid of any tensions or accidental motions (doing *nothing* well!). In this mode the seat should follow the horse's back freely, and both legs and reins are to be in constant, supple, yet *passive* contact with the horse, in a neutral, maintaining attitude.

The horse's neutral basis is a self-reliant state in which it willingly maintains the gait, rhythm, tempo, level of impulsion, bend and direction that were last delegated to it by the rider.

The giving of aids is a deliberate, *temporary* disruption of this neutral basis, and causes the desired changes in the horse's way of going or, if necessary, reconfirms that which was previously asked of the horse. The clarity of the aids is assured by keeping a sharp contrast between the *neutrality*, and the brief moments of *signalling*.

Returning to neutrality after the horse has responded correctly is also one of the most effective forms of praise. It is a consistent, logical completion of the aid, and is therefore also an ultimate justice; a virtue for which these creatures have uncanny sensitivity! We can of course further emphasize our approval by positive reinforcement: vocal praise, patting or stroking. All forms of approval are usually mirrored in the horses' greater receptiveness to further demands. I hasten to add, however, that praise should not degenerate into a form of bribery, nor become meaninglessly repetitious, in the hope that something good will come of it.

If we ignore the horse's reactions to any of our aids or movements, or to outside disturbances, the horse will gradually begin to disregard those stimuli, and will file them mentally under *'insignificant background noise'*. This principle desensitizes the horse. If this happens unintentionally to an imperceptive beginner it causes the horse to become dull and unresponsive. However, when used deliberately by an experienced rider, it can be most helpful in causing a nervous or excited horse to become calmed and mellowed. To reiterate, we can cause the horse to become settled if we learn to be *poker-faced* about all outside disturbances, (including the silly effects these may cause in the horse), and assume the attitude of, 'I can't see anything, or hear anything', while patiently, yet firmly, urging the horse to continue doing the exercises at hand. *Putting the horse to work, i.e., sending the horse forward and asking it for a specific school figure or exercise, is the best way to overcome problems of silliness, shying or inattentiveness.*

The converse principle sensitizes the horse. This too can be a blessing or a curse depending on the rider's ability to implement it deliberately. In other words, we can make a dull horse more sensitive, by noticing and reacting to every little reaction it makes. Or by the same process we can make any horse neurotic and silly by allowing ourselves to be constantly distracted and annoyed by outside disturbances, and the effects these might have in the horse (being negatively reactionary). Such matters as the 'arena door syndrome', or the 'mad rapist' in the corner! are all rider-induced problems. Of course, any horse will shy sometimes. But only through suitable rider attitudes is this minimized and quickly neutralized.

We must therefore, needless to say, be sure that we ourselves, through insensitivity, lack of tactfulness, or incorrect influences, do not perpetuate the horse's unwanted behaviour, and timid or nervous riders will first need to get a grip on their emotions before improvement can be expected from the horse.

Our natural riding tools, the hands, legs, and seat, do not work in

126

an isolated manner, but constantly interact to address the whole horse. Nevertheless, only *one active* aid should be given at any one moment. During this time the other riding tools should remain passive: containing, supporting, preventing, receiving, and yielding or allowing as necessary. All aids must work consistently and unambiguously to attain a single goal. Vague or contradictory aids can lead to nothing but confusion, confrontation, and resistance.

We must expect *and* get results promptly from every aid *every time*. Should the horse not obey, the aid is to be intensified *immediately*, and given as energetically as necessary, until the desired response comes. In a matter-of-fact way we convince the horse of the choice it should make. To neutralize our aids *before* we have achieved some response from the horse (giving up), jeopardizes our authority and control.

It is important to interject here, that the use of the concepts 'authority' and 'control' should be equated with the role of a good factory or corporation manager. One who guides the 'ship' by sheer power of personality, presence, and a thorough understanding of all phases of production. The employees work efficiently and willingly for such a person, because they are handled with tactfulness and respect: they are reasonably corrected when their work falls below par, or receive due recognition for work well done. Riding demands that we be good leaders. Here neither the hesitant, irresolute or feeble person, nor the ruthless, insensitive ogre will succeed. It is a cultivation of effective control, yet without ever abusing that privilege once that ability to control has been gained. It is the gentle power, born out of understanding, compassion and effectiveness, of which masters are made.

Back to the subject at hand. Any aid that does not elicit a response from the horse, regardless of the reason, cannot be considered an aid. Signals can only truly be considered aids when the following requirements have taken place:

1) The aid was given correctly.
2) A result was obtained. The horse has shown a degree of willingness to respond. (Depending on the horse and the

moment, sometimes a small, partial response is sufficient; at other times nothing short of a complete response is acceptable.)

3) The rider has neutralized completely after that response occurs.

GIVE AN AID; GET A RESULT; STOP GIVING THE AID.

In this way the horse is constantly tuned and retuned to the aids; a process which actually never stops, regardless of the level of training. Depending on our consistency, the horse can be tuned or dulled quite readily.

Essential to the above points, however, is the vital pre-condition that our requests are reasonable: suited to the horse's level of development, and that on any given day the horse is adequately prepared to execute the desired exercises. All aids should be carefully introduced. To ambush or surprise the horse with any request will only undermine its confidence in, and respect for, the rider. We must also be fully prepared before making demands on the horse otherwise only mediocre results can be expected.

Should the horse not be performing as well as usual, one should consider the possibility that it might be sore or not feeling well. It is often difficult to determine the cause for regression in the quality of work. If there is any uncertainty, the horse should be given the benefit of the doubt, before we 'lay down the law'. If a few days of rest do not improve the situation, a reputable instructor or veterinarian should be consulted.

THE BI-LATERAL PASSIVE REIN INFLUENCES

These influences fall into four categories: (a) the basic neutral, accepting contact; (b) the influence of passive resistance; (c) the forward-yielding rein; (d) the leading rein. A description follows.

(a) *The basic neutral contact* passively and elastically accepts the weight the horse puts in it. This encompasses the *filtering* hand, which keeps just enough energy within the horse to maintain its balance, while letting the rest out the front as forward motion.

Through the use of loosening/suppling exercises the horse must be brought to that state in which it puts equal weight in both reins. Unequal weight, or hardness in the reins, point to imbalance, tensions, or resistance in the horse (discomfort or lameness is a possibility), or may be caused by faulty, one-sided guidance by the rider.

(b) *An influence of passive resistance* is one of the attitudes used during halts or half-halts (see below). If the horse resists the bit, the hand counter-resists *passively* (that is, it neither yields forward, nor does it in any way take back) and the active driving aids must cause the horse to rebalance itself and yield to the bit once again. It must remain an elastic restraint, and should not become a hard, crass, or unfriendly snubbing-off. The hand merely interrupts the forward motion by closing the front door, more or less. When using this influence the rider must ensure that the balance and forward tendency of the horse are maintained by the seat and legs.

(c) *The forward yielding rein* is used to lengthen the horse's frame during extensions of the gaits, forward and downward stretching, and in preparation for riding on the loose rein. The horse's frame should always be lengthened by the driving aids.

(d) *The leading influence of the inside rein* is temporarily used to guide young horses onto a circle from a straight line. *This is in no way a bending influence!* The inside rein may be 'opened', that is, it can be brought away from the horse's withers and neck by about 6–10 inches. This is strictly a passive influence, and the rider may not pull back; it is a guiding rein, and only that. With more advanced horses the inside rein can also 'guide', but in this case it isn't necessary to open the rein away from the neck.

The hands should never work backward actively. The only times the hands may come backward at all is when they *passively follow* the horse's head back (to avoid losing the contact) as it shortens its frame from the effects of half-halts, halts, when putting the horse 'on the aids', when collecting the horse, or when bending, all of which are achieved and fulfilled by the active driving aids.

THE UNILATERAL ACTIVE REIN INFLUENCES

There are two unilateral active rein influences: the active checking aid, and the active bending aid (caution!! read below).

The active checking aid can be used during halts, and half-halts, and consists of a nudging on the outside rein with the fingers. This influence is given within the hand only, as opposed to using the whole arm. Active rein aids should only be used *deliberately* and *momentarily*, and should not degenerate into a constant fiddling with the bit. Though stronger checks might occasionally have to be used, they should only be given *from within a contact*.

It is essential to understand that any active rein aids can only achieve a suitable and correct response when the horse is coming up to the bit from behind (stretching for it) and is adequately supple and 'on the aids'. If the horse is at all tense anywhere in its body, active rein aids will only confirm or worsen that tension. *A horse must be supple and permeable before active rein aids of any kind can be usefully implemented* (035, completion of the circuit).

Harsh rein aids are no substitute for correct, patient training. If horses are stiff, or are lugging on the bit, it is usually a sign of imbalance or resistance, neither of which can be cured by any direct, active action of the hand. A kind, elastic, passive, *waiting* hand, in combination with using careful active driving aids, while doing suppling exercises is the only correct solution.

THE BENDING AIDS

The main purpose of the bending aids is to help supple the horse so that it can better execute the rider's wishes. Only through bending and suppleness can true straightness be achieved. Straightness not only encompasses the accurate following of the hind legs in the same path of the front legs, but includes a *clearing of the channel*, from back to front, of all obstructions – tensions and resistance – so that the forward energy can arrive unimpeded and evenly to both sides of the bit. Bending is the key to getting the horse to carry itself equally on lateral pairs of legs. The sign that correct bending and suppling have

130

been attained, is that the horse's back becomes easy to sit on, that it is soft and even on both reins, and that it is not bulging against or leaning on either or the rider's legs. (Important: see section 028–B for detailed description of bending).

THE LEG AIDS

The leg aids can only become effective when both seat bones are firmly anchored to the saddle, and when both knees are closed in light contact with the saddle flaps.

The rider must tune the horse sufficiently to the legs that it responds promptly to the smallest signals. Riders often rely far too much on physical strength to push the horse forward, or to cause it to yield to sideways pressure. This practice generally only leads to cramping and tensions in both horse and rider. It is a clear sign that the horse is not correctly on the aids.

Though it might *occasionally* be necessary to use stronger aids during training, this is only productive when it results in the horse responding to lighter signals immediately afterwards – a momentary enforcement to put the point across. Riding with strength continually can never achieve a good relationship with the horse, nor produce the ease and elegance which is associated with a higher quality of horsemanship. On the one hand we have only ignorant, brute coercion; on the other, we have refined guidance which is based on sanity, sensitivity, and equestrian tact.

In any gait the animating aids from the legs can either be active or passive. The passive aids are given by applying a steady increase of pressure, held for as much as several strides, with both legs equally (squeezing a tube of toothpaste). The active aid encompasses a nudging or vibrating with the inside leg at the trot and canter, while the outside leg gives the same pressure passively. At the walk, both legs may animate actively with alternate left-right aids, as the horse's corresponding hind foot is about to come off the ground.

Whenever a strong animating influence is wanted in the trot or canter, both legs may be used *actively*, it is an exception, however. Satisfactory animating influences from the legs cannot be achieved without correct *engagement* of the seat. The leg (stick, or spur) tunes the horse to the influences of the seat. Ultimately, the seat should become the principal guiding (aiding) influence.

Lateral yielding responses are attained by an increase of pressure in only one of the rider's legs, for exercises such as turns on the forehand, leg-yielding, and shoulder-in. During the early training phases of either horse or rider, the yielding leg may be brought back by about five or six inches from its normal position. In the more advanced stages, good lateral effects should be obtained with the rider's yielding leg at the girth. The yielding leg may have to be active – an 'on-off' pressure given in time with the stepping of the horse's corresponding hind leg. Ideally, however, the horse should be taught to move willingly away from the slightest increase of pressure *passively applied* by either leg.

During any yielding work both reins are to have equal pressure. Their only duty is to supervise the bend and the correct rhythm/tempo, while quietly stabilizing the base of the horse's neck onto the withers and shoulders. *One is strictly to refrain from causing sideways yielding through any tugging on one of the reins.* Only obedience to the seat and legs will result in acceptable work. The correctness of yielding exercises can be tested by riding with both reins in one hand.

Any time the leg aids, honestly and correctly given, do not obtain adequate responses from the horse, they should be enforced immediately with either whip or spurs. A note of caution, however: horses can readily be dulled or spoiled by these sharpening instruments if indiscretely (over) used.

During work on circles or bent lines, should the horse not obey the passive containing role of the outside leg, which would prevent the quarters from swinging out, that leg may be made active briefly to assert its presence.

In concluding, our communication with the horse would be sadly incomplete if we were only to ensure the austere technical perfection of our signalling system. In order to bring the full potential of our influence on the horse to bear, the aids should be transmitted on a wave-length of sound equestrian philosophy; a foundation of attitudes nurtured by lengthy steeping in an environment where the

132

rider is exposed to examples of excellence in all phases of horseman-ship, whereby these can gradually permeate the rider's very core – absorbed through his pores, as it were.

If we are genuinely dedicated to achieving classical work, that is, striving for total harmony with the horse's nature, we must learn to appeal to the horse's psyche, and come to understand it as fully as possible. Thus we raise our work from a strictly physical, technical manipulation, to a dignified plane of intelligent communication which engages our whole being. We succeed not because we have thwarted the horse at its own game, but because we have united with it in a greater goal of understanding and co-operation; a triumph in which the horse is respected, and in which it both willingly and fully takes part.

The unmistakeable essence which radiates from correct work is that the rider is no longer merely sitting either on or in the horse, but that the horse appears stuck under the rider's seat, as though suspended from a large electro-magnet. Collected canter, left.

CHAPTER IX

ELEMENTS OF THE DRESSAGE SEAT

To talk about the seat means to talk about all of horsemanship – a total influence, a mastery of self, a philosophy of riding encompassing respect for the horse, and a comprehensive understanding of its nature.

Studying the workings of the seat, an elusive quantity at best, can be compared in certain ways to the modern-day study of sub-atomic particles. Just as these can only be partially understood through their interactions and effects upon other elements and forces, so too the seat can only be understood through its effects on the horse. One can certainly establish fairly good approximations of how to attain satisfactory results from the seat/position, but it would be a staggeringly futile undertaking to explain in detail the myriad seat adjustments required during any one riding session, these being relevant only to that particular horse, rider and moment in time. Only personal experience can begin to divulge the rainbow of nuances meaningfully to each rider.

The purpose of this chapter is to present an outline of those practical conditions under which correct elements of the seat can develop. It is only when such development has taken place that an effective influence can be brought to bear by the rider, this in turn resulting in a living state of harmony with the horse.

Fundamentally, it is the seat's function to transmit and receive all messages. *But the seat itself is the message (!)*; it must therefore be constantly drawn into a ribbon of accord, reeling-off harmoniously and articulately as the horse moves.

It is a paradoxical and somewhat disconcerting fact, considering the great effort required to develop an effective seat, that ideal harmony is actually a gift of circumstance, and comes to the rider only in small, jewel-like moments over the years. This is so because harmony between two living creatures cannot be dictated, but must be willed to come about by each participant. At best we can strive to make circumstances such that harmony has the greatest chance of occurring.

Though certain technicalities must be mastered before a good seat can evolve, ideal seat attitudes are a result of intuition and automatic reactions which must be roundly served by adequate, correct experience. This might be compared to the development of a goalkeeper's skill, who through his accumulated experience and intuition, and not just reflexes, narrows his chances of being scored against. Sensitivity, keen intuition, and correct habits can equally give the rider the best opportunity to react suitably to any given situation.

For unspoiled horses, and those without unsuitable temperaments, obedience to the influences of a correct seat is inescapable. This is so because correct signalling addresses the natural forces of physics, affecting the very nub of the creature's make-up – its sense of well-being and self-preservation – its balance. It is one of the foremost goals of horsemanship however, that not only horse and rider be individually balanced, but that their centres of balance should coincide. In this synchronized state the rider's slightest influences come right home, their effects being strongly amplified, whereby the rider can start to 'play' the horse effortlessly at the tip of his seat-wand. The horse becomes subject to the rider, and the rider subject to the horse; neither can any longer make any motions without fully taking into account the other.

Horses are masters at communicating via subtle physical gesture; to them it is simple foal's play, they do it all the time. It is little wonder they can perform so beautifully to the 'invisible' seat aids. Yet, before the rider can enter into this world of fine-spun communication, the seat must become quiet, and free of unwanted, or unintentional, movements in the saddle.

To attain the basic quietness, balance, and independence of the seat can take an able-bodied rider about three years, provided one has had correct guidance. However, assimilating a viable, rich equine vocabulary, and an articulate mode of expression – cultivating an *educated seat* – is a never-ending task. Furthermore, it is also essential for the aspiring rider to develop suppleness, agility, and physical fitness, without which, quality horsemanship is unthinkable.

There are three inseparable prerequisites that constitute the seat:

(a) The rider's position.
(b) Control over the attitudes of the lower back and pelvis.
(c) The ability to cause the horse to arrive at a supple, balanced, and 'carrying' state.

Let us analyse the first two aspects in detail. The last point encompasses the accumulative understanding of all aspects of working the horse correctly, and is described throughout this book.

The purpose of the rider's work on his position must be the achievement of functionality through the deliberate placing of all body parts into the most favourable attitude. In this way balance and control of the horse can be achieved with minimum physical effort on the rider's part. If the rider's seat and position are correct, the horse will go correctly.

There are no short-cuts for the initial hard work, nor any skirting of the pains which must be endured in acquiring a viable position. Those who believe that one can first learn to 'get the horse going', and only later paste-on a pleasing position artificially, are doomed to failure. Without his major work-tool, a functional and correct position, the rider is left no choice but to resort to false influences which become ingrained habits, very hard to eradicate later. Such contrived influences have little impact on the natural forces of the horse other than to disrupt them. Only through the initial technical correctness of the position is the potential for effective aiding established.

Going to the opposite extreme, however, of concentrating solely on position correctness to the exclusion of constant analytical sensing of its effects on the horse, can only fashion an ineffectual 'glass-cabinet ornament', which must somehow be maintained despite the jarring motion of the horse.

The attitudes of the lower back and seat are aimed singularly at achieving accurate control over the fall of the rider's weight into the seat bones. Though these attitudes have a decisive impact in the giving of aids, the actual physical alterations in the rider to affect these weight influences are very minute, and become quite useless when exaggerated. It is a powerful, yet subtle, tool!

The two major influences of the lower back and seat affect:

(a) Directional guidance of the horse through the increased loading of one of the seat bones. This unilateral weight aid must be harmoniously augmented by correct bending aids, and by letting a bit more weight flow through the inside heel.

(b) A greater or lesser driving influence attained by the bilateral weight aid: increasing or decreasing the concentration of weight in both seat bones simultaneously.

The greatest problems in learning what 'driving' and its phantom partner 'bracing the back' is all about, lies in the tendency, so often the case, to latch onto some isolated highlights of theoretical advice, and all but to ignore the fine nuances which are at least as important. This results in the most monstrous distortions of what was originally perfectly sound advice. Riders end up looking like bear-wrestlers, with backs hunched, chests collapsed, and not infrequently leaning backward while the seat is held forward and under in an exaggerated way. They literally try to shove their horses forward physically, stride after stride, with gross, active gyrations of the pelvis in the saddle. Not only are these attitudes hideously unsightly, but their forceful nature prevents the horse from using its powers freely. These are certainly not the elements of grace and effortlessness which mark the valid classical seat.

The absolute pinnacle to which the rider should aspire is to develop a seat/position which is absolutely quiet in relation to the horse's back. Any additional active motion in the rider, beyond that which is caused through being moved by the horse, is most undesirable. Certainly, rounding the back, or leaning backward with a 'pushing' attitude, reaps no positive benefit at all. There are those few exceptions in which the rider may lean back *slightly* and *momentarily*: when urging a particularly resistant 'withholding' (or bucking) horse forward, or when making a downward transition from a strong trot or canter to the halt. In this last case it only appears as

138

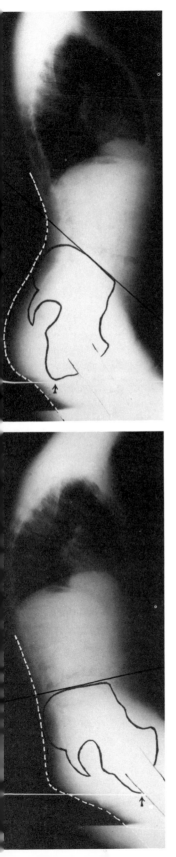

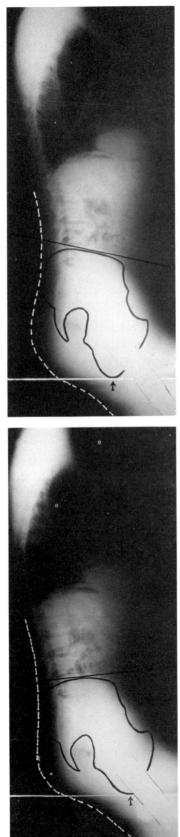

On this page is a series of actual X-rays of the Author's position, which clarify the various attitudes of the pelvis and back. The horizontal white line represents the flat surface upon which the seat bones rest. The pelvis is outlined in black. The arrow locates the weight-bearing points of the seat bones. The thigh bone is lightly outlined. The broken white line marks the 7 flesh extremities of the back. The transverse black line shows the tilt of the pelvis.

Top left
Hollow back. This common fault is often seen with the upper body leaning forward or backward.

Top right
Correct normal seat.

Bottom left
Hunched back. This incorrect attitude is frequently misconstrued as a bracing. The upper body is completely collapsed, the weight is dissipated and cannot be effectively concentrated into the seat bones.

Bottom right
Shows the correct effects of pelvic tilt (holding the pubic crest forward). This is emphasized especially when driving, or bracing the back.

139

though the rider is leaning back (relative to the ground), but as long as the rider's spine remains perpendicular to the horse's back (dictated by the maintenance of balance) it is perfectly acceptable.

Any leaning back during the bulk of ordinary work smacks of a forceful attitude that point to the following problems:

- Hanging onto the horse's mouth.
- A lack of balance and independence of the upper body and hands.
- Being left behind the motion.
- Trapping the horse between the seat and hands.

The notion that one needs to drive continuously is also erroneous. The rider must learn to generate a certain, necessary level of impulsion, enough to achieve balance and fluid forward motion (putting the horse correctly 'on the aids') and then *delegate* the task of maintaining that energy level to the horse. The rider then, as control centre, only needs to monitor the horse's performance, and interject when necessary with short, energetic driving aids, just sufficient to remind the horse to uphold its end of the bargain.

If the seat is incorrect, the energy level depletes readily (imagine a leaky car tyre), the necessary pressure in the horse, that is, its forward desire and balance, cannot be maintained, and must be regenerated time and time again. This is both needlessly tiring and wholly ineffective riding that can only produce dull or soured horses. Unless the rider improves the quality of the seat he will be forced to resort to excessive use of stick or spurs, resulting in a vicious circle of intensified and multiplied giving of aids, instead of, ideally, causing the horse to respond to ever fewer and lighter aids. *Let the horse do the work!*

How are the correct driving attitudes of the seat attained? First let's review the essential position requirements:

- The head must be held upright, chin lightly drawn in, look to the horizon.
- The upper body must be truly vertical (balanced), quiet and stretched; poised, athletically toned.

- The shoulders must be drawn back lightly (open the top of the chest), and allowed to hang down.
- The stomach muscles should generally be supple and be allowed to hang towards the hands. (See below, bracing.)
- The front line of the upper body should be made as long as possible (a well raised chest, *not forced*). (See photo on page 120.)
- The lower back should be only very slightly hollowed and remain supple (the whole spine making a flattened 'S' shape).
- Most of the rider's weight should be carried equally on both seat bones; a small amount should be borne on the crotch (the pubic crest, the third point of support).
- The legs and relaxed thighs must be fully turned inward from the hip, to allow the weight to fall freely into the seat bones, and towards the ground via lowered heels.
- Imagine riding with the shins, not with the back of the calf or the heels.
- The knees should be kept closed in light contact with the saddle flaps.

We must take it as a basic premise that during all riding the muscles should be correctly used with supple contractions and relaxations. Any hard cramping or spastic contraction, contortion, or stiffness anywhere in one's body is most undesirable, and is a major impediment to correct influences and results. However, suppleness or relaxation does not mean sloppiness!

The correct driving attitude of the seat/position consists of three entirely separate, yet interacting, factors:

(a) Stretching the whole position from head to heel.
(b) Holding the seat bones well forward.
(c) Bracing the back.

Let us analyse each of these factors in detail.

The stretching of the position is a readily understood concept for any rider; think of sitting taller, more erect, growing upward, having a 'regal bearing', etc. It serves to consolidate the whole body whereby the rider gains accurate control of balance and the precise 'fall of

141

weight' into the seat bones. Without this stretching, the upper body is too sloppy, and the rider's weight is dissipated, rendering its potential effects void. The stretching effect must also be carried all the way down through the heels towards the ground.

Holding the seat bones and pubic crest well forward, is achieved by a rotation of the pelvis around its axis, the hip joint. This is called 'pelvic tilt'. It causes the lower back to flatten somewhat. It is this attitude which brings the rider to sit *'over the knee'*, whereby the weight energy can flow down through the leg and to the ground. It is important to interject here that regardless of how emphatically the pubic crest is held forward, the rider's weight must always go straight down into the saddle (no leaning back). Furthermore, any of these pelvic adjustments should not be exaggerated. *Pelvic tilt is an attitude, purely and simply, and nothing more!*

One should be able to achieve this rotation of the pelvis without tightening the stomach muscles, which should remain merely *elastically toned* most of the time. Riding with tense stomach muscles cramps the upper body, impedes free relaxed breathing, and makes it difficult to get the desired length of the front line with a free, open, and raised chest (the filled, billowing sail).

The pelvic tilt attitude causes the rider's centre of mass to go down into the hips (as opposed to being in the upper torso), which promotes greater stability of the rider's body. Furthermore, this attitude is fundamental in maintaining the energy we have generated in the horse (impulsion, balance), and helps the rider to keep the horse in front of the seat and leg.

Bracing the back is, first of all, one of the essential aspects of the driving influences when used in conjunction with 'stretching', 'pelvic tilt' and the driving leg aid. Secondly, through bracing the back, the hand finds the necessary base for support or resistance in the seat. Thus, when bracing is used in conjunction with such rein resistance, and with the active or passive driving aids from the legs, it causes the horse to react in a 'gathering' or collecting fashion; causing a more pronounced engagement of the hind legs towards the centre of balance, and a deeper flexion of the three major joints of its hind legs (hip, stifle, and hock) which become more mobile and springy. This is the nucleus of the half-halt, the prime avenue to balancing the horse. (052, half-halt.)

For want of better words, the rider brings about the attitude or 'action' of bracing (it is a *steady, passive influence*), by *thinking* of pushing the small of the lower back FORWARD (think of it as being the *top* of the pelvis), while emphasizing the lengthening of the front line of the upper body, and maintaining the pelvic tilt mentioned earlier. That which appears to be confusing is that the rider should in no way actually hollow the lower back while this is being done. It is a clear *attitude* of pushing the lower back forward without in any way altering the 'pelvic tilt'. The seat bones continue to be held under and forward by pelvic tilt, *but the focus of the energy while bracing lies in the passive, forward pushing of the small of the back*. Bracing, therefore, should in no way alter the outward appearance of the rider's body or position. Regardless of the intensity of the bracing, the seat must always remain elastic and harmonious with the movement of the horse's back (no cramping or stiffness).

Slight bracing influences, such as might be used during general driving, may be used continuously; as long as the horse remains 'driveable' (023), and its back compliant. Not only is bracing an essential part of such a driving influence, but it helps the seat remain glued to the horse's back. Bracing the back is to be employed with sensitivity and tactfulness, the rider always listening to the horse in order to measure the exact amount that might be necessary and acceptable as each moment requires. Strong bracing influences, which might be used while 'tuning' the horse to the driving aids, for example, should only be used very briefly. For use during half-halts, the duration and intensity of bracing should be commensurate to the amount of resistance needed in the reins at any given moment, and should last only as long as that resistance is necessary, seldom more than a stride or two. As with all things one must find the happy medium. When the back is braced too briefly, or not strongly enough, it will not cause the horse to react adequately to the rein's resistance. Used too long or too strongly, its effects are negated because the horse can readily learn to drop its back or stiffen it against the rider (instead of becoming better balanced, and more springy in the hindquarters) in order to free itself from such an overbearing, unyielding influence.

Thus to recapitulate briefly:

(a) Stretching produces the rider's carriage or bearing. It consolidates the upper body and gives the rider a practical, useful form, assisting in the control over his weight and balance. It is used most of the time, but is especially emphasized during halts, half-halts, transitions, etc.

(b) Pelvic tilt holds the seat bones and pubic crest more or less emphatically forward, while allowing the lower back and upper body the freedom to follow and flow with the horse's movements. It is used more or less most of the time, and assists the rider in keeping the horse in front of the seat and leg. This too is emphasized while driving, and during halts, half-halts, and transitions.

(c) The bracing of the back is central to the driving influences, and also provides the reins with a base for support or resistance, which is hereby transferred via the seat to the horse's back. Slight bracing influences, such as might be needed for general driving, may be used continuously. Stronger bracing, used during halts, half-halts, and transitions, or while tuning the horse, should only be used temporarily, and varies in duration and intensity as needed.

As long as we recognize these three major seat functions as being individual aspects, and learn to orchestrate them harmoniously, each with precisely the right proportion, in time success will be ours. The suitability of the attitudes of the seat and position should be solely measured by the correctness of their influence on the horse.

Those aspects of horsemanship that are hopelessly shrouded to all who have not exposed themselves to critical equestrian study, become plainly self-evident to the rider who has achieved self-mastery, and has taken the time to cultivate a high quality seat and position. The years of ardent work finally surrender their most cherished fruit: the liberation of the horse, which now senses the

144

freedom of its powers, and begins to carry the rider proudly and lightly on its supple back with graceful, cadenced movements.

The rider senses a joyous and deep inner serenity emanating from the true harmony that has been found with another living creature. It is a home-coming – the ultimate prize, reaped from this prince of riding instruments – the seat.

Oberbereiter Meixner, Levade.

CHAPTER X

THOUGHTS ON THE NATURE OF ART

Nature does not hide her secrets by way or ruse, but because she is so essentially lofty. Albert Einstein.

INTRODUCTION

The subject of this final chapter has been broached because of the fairly common and indiscriminate use of the title, '*The Classical Art of Riding*', to describe almost any dressage, irrespective, it seems, of its actual quality. Indeed, not all dressage riding attains artistic spheres. In the following study, therefore, I have tried to identify those elements which should be present before a work might be considered an art at all.

It may surprise the reader to find that this essay is not restricted solely to classical riding, but that it casts its net far afield in search of the most fundamental essences of art in general. This has been done because I believe that all art forms must share a common basis. Thus, if that universal foundation can be delineated, we will possibly be able to see more clearly not only what makes art art, but also under what circumstances High School riding could be considered to take its rightful place among aesthetic art works.

A SHADOW OF ART

In step with force of forces
      Dancing
Work of hands
      Entranced
The medium fashioned
      To life now trembles
      Gift of circumstance.

In mind's deep forest
      Self absented
Witness to participant
      Transforms
And there among the boughs
      Discovers
Such beauty as truth adorns.

Its strange familiar aires
      Composing
      Primal Cosmic bars
As the bow of toil
      Faint tremor draws
From strings
      That play the stars.

By art's elixir now trilling
      One
Embraced the Love
      That lit the Sun.

The apostle Phillip. Leonardo da Vinci. Study sketch for his fresco 'The Last Supper'.

A STUDY OF THE PROPERTIES AND CIRCUMSTANCES OF ART

Besides the controversial subjects of religion and politics, few topics come to mind that can elicit more lively discussion than those which tangle with the elusive nature of art. This is particularly so if we consider that the word *art* has been used to describe almost every human toil, ranging anywhere from Rembrandt's masterpieces to skinning a fish! Well then, we might ask ourselves, what actually does constitute art?

Certainly the word 'art', in its broadest sense, could indeed apply to many of man's works and products, provided these are of the highest quality. But for the sake of analysis, I have divided this topic into two basic categories: functional, and aesthetic art.

Functional or technical art entails those things which fulfil our practical needs – utensils, instruments, furniture, bridges, build-ings, cars, ships, aircraft, and innumerable handicrafts, and, of course, 'art' has also come to imply the craftsman's knack or skill in being able to make or do things extremely well.

Aesthetic or fine art, which is the main subject of this essay, drifts into the metaphysical realm of life. Under this heading we find sculpture, painting, music and poetry. Also included are the per-forming arts, such as ballet, figure skating, acting, and classical riding. The cultivation and expression of the human spirit is the chief quality of this category. The physical and wholly practical give way to the tenuous and spiritual.

Though functional and aesthetic art have been arbitrarily separ-ated here, a sharp line of division does not actually exist between them. Rather, they could be seen as occupying opposite extremes of an imaginary 'art scale', overlapping and merging into one another imperceptibly, somewhere in the middle, where they combine to form a pleasing whole with both practical as well as aesthetic appeal:

150

a beautiful dress, building, automobile, hand-painted china, or any artistic ornamentation of practical things.

What might further distinguish aesthetic art from its sibling, functional art?

Is aesthetic art not a work of beauty, an inspired act, through which the artist expresses his joy and admiration for the object of his love? Is it not an affirmation of life; an ultimate statement of humanness generated through the disciplined energy of the whole person – body and soul? Is this tenuous quality not precisely that which separates an ordinary handicraft from a masterpiece: that it transcends the confines of three-dimensional time and space, and finds its reflection deep within archetypal cosmic essences? Are these not the attributes that have conferred to art its timeless quality, whereby it has leaped beyond ideologies, fashions, boundaries and cultures over the ages – making it truly the common idiom of all mankind?

Which qualities might a person need to be able to produce aesthetic art? Some of the basic requirements include technical skill, physical dexterity and, most importantly, artistic talent. Let's have a closer look at what talent might be.

Talent is an inborn ability. Everybody has a degree of talent in some area of the vast spectrum of human activity: athletic, managerial, mechanical, philosophical, etc. Each endeavour requires its own special aptitude, and must be nurtured and developed if its full potential is to be realized. Talent ranges anywhere from fairly common mild levels to the rare orbits of genius.

That talent which pertains to the production of aesthetic art is measured by the degree of an individual's perceptive sensitivity for, and ability to harmonize with, the physical and spiritual workings of nature. One who is gifted with artistic talent, is guided by a gut-feeling or intuitive knowledge: a subconscious spontaneity which synthesizes the conscious intentions of the artist as the spiritual and material fabric of art are woven into a work of beauty.

The greatest of technical skills without artistic talent will only result in a handicraft – technically perfect, yet sterile and lifeless, without any significant qualities beyond its face value. Nonetheless, it is highly improbable if not impossible for exceptional art to be

151

produced without such technical skill. It is interesting to note that some works which are not entirely technically perfect can still radiate considerable aesthetic charm. There would be an inherent danger in taking such a phenomenon as a basic guide, however, because the concept of 'freedom of expression' would most assuredly break down if the artist were erringly to equate this with freedom from discipline. Because only the full mastery of technicalities, (which should grow side by side with the flowering of talent) enables the artist to manipulate his medium effortlessly, and allows the desired expression to flow, being unimpeded by the limitations of physical awkwardness. In this way talent is fully liberated and finds its wings.

When considering those qualities central to good art, none stands out more prominently than beauty. In fact, beauty seems to encompass all other significant aspects of art within it. Is it not through the evocative power of beauty that we are inspired and uplifted. Surely a work which lacks in this essential element cannot attain the domain of aesthetic art.

Though our first impulse might be to consider beauty an entirely subjective matter, upon closer scrutiny, we can discover that it is possible to establish a fairly objective evaluation if we endeavour to seek a guiding authority beyond ourselves.

What is beauty? Beauty finds its origins in the core of the Creator Spirit of the universe: the furnace of nature's mighty laws and forces to which all existence hums in perfect obedience. Its natural precepts and elements have been set down at the birth of time, and exist with or without our recognition or approval. Its constants are always there, waiting for us to discover and understand them.

Beauty is an attribute that cannot be abstracted from the object which possesses it, but rather, must be wholly intrinsic within it. If something is to be beautiful it must be true to its own nature. That is, it should have a deep-rooted harmony with natural law; be in accord with its environment, and radiate a purity and authenticity to the innermost core of its being. One could say that beauty is synonymous with quintessential harmony and truth. It manifests itself as practical or functional beauty – a well made utensil or tool; physical beauty – a lovely face or beautiful form, or in graceful, elegant, fluid motion;

152

and last, spiritual beauty – outstanding virtues of personality or character. These forms can be found singly or in any combination of these.

The nub of our ability to detect beauty lies in an inborn sense for recognizing harmony in nature. We have this primal intuition because we are as much a part and product of nature as all the creatures on earth and all the stars in the heavens. One might say we are the reflective molecules of the universe. We are therefore also inescapably subject to the natural laws that govern both our physical and spiritual existence. It is this basal heritage which affords us the intuitive beacon which guides our judgement; provided, of course, it has not been clouded by preconceptions or warped by contrived doctrine. Truth from the mouths of babes!

These points are not intended to be dismissive about the very real factor of personal taste. Thankfully, beauty manifests itself in many varied ways, enough to satisfy the infinitive diversity of individual preference. Yet, only by honing our perceptive awareness, and gaining adequate experience with specific art forms, will a more mature and objective evaluation develop. This will allow us to recognize and appreciate a broader spectrum of fine art treasures, even though they might not always be of our personal taste. One may, for example, genuinely admire the paintings of seventeenth century Dutch masters, yet prefer not to have them hanging on one's walls at home.

Taking into account the properties of beauty, and the faculties we possess for recognizing them, we can readily see how these should be an integral and essential part of the production of fine art. Each work should reflect just such deep-rooted accord with nature's laws. This is embodied in its balance, its purity of rhythm, the harmony of its tonality, the fluidity of its motion, and the excellence of its proportion.

But taking us beyond these measurable qualities through the deft mediation of the artist, the work must resonate its inherent cosmic truth in the very core of our soul. This inscrutable element, which so grips us, entails the very reason for art's existence – being mankind's fascination with the intricacies of life, and its insatiable desire to

154

come to understand them. It is a yearning to find harmony with our roots.

This deeper causal aspect exists because, to create a work of fine art demands of us that we come to understand, directly or intuitively, the nature of both our medium and subject. For unless we work within the structures of the nature of both – being in harmony with their truths – we will surely fail to achieve the higher ideals of artistic expression.

The very act of finding harmony with the nature of one's art indirectly opens the doors to finding harmony with all of nature combined. And as the inner eye of our soul recognizes the fundamental truths it beholds, we experience a sublime state, an ecstasy that sets our physical and spiritual senses alight with joy. Through such delightful snippets of insight we come to a better understanding of the nature of life itself, though this might be a wholly intuitive and undefinable insight.

How do these general observations apply to the subject of this book, horsemanship?

In the art of High School riding, as with the other performing arts such as ballet or ice-dancing, ultimate performances only become possible once harmony is found with the laws of physics that govern the dynamic equilibrium of a moving body. Only then can personal expression be transmitted, to be combined into an exhilarating, fluid performance of beauty in motion.

The rider, however, has a double duty on his hands. Not only must he develop a refined mastery over his own mind and body, but he must achieve as perfect a control as possible over the horse as well. The indispensible aspect of physical unity with the horse is unattainable, however, without an initial 'meeting of minds'. This spiritual union is based on respect, trust, good will, and mutual co-operation. Any strictly technical, physical, or forceful manipulations of the creature never attain genuinely artistic performances, but rather only result in clever 'handicrafts'. The rider should, therefore, strive only to direct or guide. The *apparent* control achieved is, in effect, a true manifestation of the horse's own willingness, through conditioning and understanding, to comply with its rider's guiding requests. For it too recognizes universal law, and senses pleasure from working harmoniously with its rider.

By subjecting himself wholly to the natural laws that govern the horse, man's intellect can judiciously contribute the disciplined gymnastic training (that which the horse does not have without man's intervention) which develops the creature's athletic potential, whereby it can begin to move with the grace, balance, and suppleness of a dancer while carrying the rider.

Only after many years of relentless searching for and working in accordance with the horse's truths, does an equestrian concert eventually ensue, in which man and creature are joyfully united in purest harmony. Their performance, suffused with suppleness and verve, is presented with playful ease. This, and only this, when honestly achieved, can be considered to have attained *classical* ideals, and can be labelled *aesthetic art*.

The rider must take care not to be tempted into believing that art is only produced when doing the advanced movements. Art can exist at any level, regardless of the simplicity or complexity of the work. A grand prix ride can most definitely be lacking in any vestige of art. Conversely, a first level ride can embrace art fully. An analogy can be drawn between horsemanship and a sketch or oil painting. A good sketch (rudimentary levels of riding) is a skeleton which must contain all vital essences of the subject matter. And the oil painting (the advanced levels of riding) is an expansion in the dynamic range of those basic essences through the added dimensions of colour, hue and tonality.

To be an artist is to answer an irresistible calling – a vocation based on a sense of self-conviction. It is not motivated by ambitions for notoriety or material riches, nor is it a yielding to the pressures of popular demand. It is a dedication of one's life to the simplicity of the daily task, born out of a singular, invincible urge to attain excellence, and the fulfilment of a talent that cannot be denied. This is unfalsifiable, for only in the truth of one's product – its honesty and good quality – lies the foundation of one's authority to be called an artist.

When the artist escapes his bonds, and soars into the spaceless halls of unselfconsciousness, the finest of works are born. Fleeting glimpses of creative inspiration, as though of their own accord, opportunely coincide with flowing moments of skillfulness. Spirit and matter merge, and are transformed into a delicate substance which radiates a life of its own – a life which is greater than the work or the participants involved – it becomes a celebration of all of creation.

Ever a catalyst to thought and searching, art teases and awakens our curiosity as it exposes the compelling intricacies of universal workings. And so we are drawn unwittingly into the wondrous gardens of life's mysteries, where we are touched by the ineffable and the intangiable – it is art.

CLOSING THOUGHTS

Just what is in store for classical riding in these times? Ours is indeed a trying era, one in which we are incessantly accosted by frivolity, numbed by sensationalism, and seduced by the easy voice of instant gratification. It seems that solutions are readily and painlessly available for all of our problems or dreams. We have become so crafty at producing imitations of every kind, that we have become blunted, and no longer appear to miss things of real value. So long as it *looks* good, that's all that seems to matter!

The art of riding does not find its home easily in such modern-day philosophy. Here there is no space for synthetics. The horse does not understand how to be anything other than itself. Its nature will not be hurried. Yet, God only knows, the wiles of humanity respect no bounds. For centuries riders have attempted to find shortcuts to training the horse. And by the token of 'if one can wag a dog's tail for it it will be happy', riders have forced the horse into taking on baseless *symptoms* of correct work, with blatant indifference for its well-being. Unavoidably, such riders fall victim to their own contrivances, and begin to believe that these perversions of the horse actually result in a valid product. The connoisseur, however, looks straight through the shallow glitter of the pretender's 'High School movements', and recognizes the tense, broken gaits, and the defeated spirit of the horse.

Let us dare to look the fact straight in the eye. Regardless of the real or imagined qualifications of the rider in the saddle, neither this author, nor any riding instructor, nor all the masters past or present, if these are, or ever wish to be known as true horsemen, are worth the air they breathe unless they subject – no, *surrender* – themselves unconditionally to the nature of the horse. If the horse does not reflect in its work that it has become truly more beautiful because of man's intervention,[1] the work is, quite simply, not up to classical standards.

What refinement we must cultivate in order to earn the right to help in the development of the equine ballerina. It is a grave responsibility indeed. One which foremost requires of us that we humble ourselves in the sanctuary of the horse. Let us put aside all petty self-interest, and all work that is not friendly or considerate to this most noble of creatures, and build our horsemanship and our lives, with which it is fully entwined, on substantial fundamental values. For only from such a sound basis can we fully explore the dynamic breadth of this subject, and forge the coveted equestrian union without in any way diminishing the most beautiful aspects of being human for the rider, and of being and remaining fully 'equine' for the horse.

Egon von Neindorff places the following incisive question before us, 'What will we have left behind for posterity?'

Let us resolve to answer that question by exemplifying in our daily actions our respect for nature, and accept, each and every one of us, our duty to bear the living equestrian torch. To nurture it lovingly while it is in our stewardship. And to pass it on unstintingly and undiminished to all those who wish to share in its fruits. For our own self-worth, let us strive to make our work as honest and real as we possibly can. That thereby it may become inspiring and uplifting by the sheer power of its elemental beauty – and become the sound edifice for future generations to build on and to enjoy.

The horses will remain our true and ultimate judges, let us always listen to them.

---

[1] Indicated by its mental calmness and acceptance, and the correctness of its muscular development which blossoms due to its supple, active, balanced, and pure gaits. (059, 060, and Chapter 7).

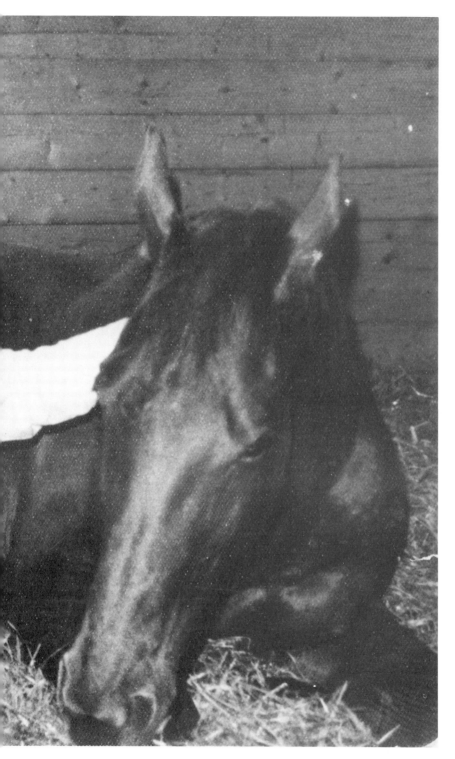

PHOTO BY J. G. HERBERMANN

RECOMMENDED READING:

- *Riding Logic*, Wilhelm Museler.
- *Horsemanship*, Waldimar Seunig.
- *Dressage Riding*, Richard L. Watjen.
- *The Inner Game of Tennis*, W. Timothy Gallwey.